A Time to Dance

Ohio History and Culture

A Time to Dance

The Life of Heinz Poll

Heinz Poll

Edited by Barbara Schubert

The University of Akron Press

Akron, Ohio

All rights reserved • First Edition 2008 • Manufactured in the United States of America.
• All inquiries and permission requests should be addressed to the Publisher, The
University of Akron Press, Akron, Ohio 44325-1703.
www.uakron.edu/uapress

12 11 10 09 08 5 4 3 2 1

LIBRARY OF CONGRESS CATALOGING-IN-PUBLICATION DATA
Poll, Heinz.
A time to dance : the life of Heinz Poll / by Heinz Poll; edited by Barbara Schubert.
p. cm.
ISBN 978-1-931968-51-5 (cloth : alk. paper)—ISBN 978-1-931968-52-2 (pbk. : alk. paper)
1. Poll, Heinz. 2. Choreographers—Germany—Biography. 3. Ohio Ballet—History.
I. Schubert, Barbara, 1939– II. Title.
GV1785.P63A3 2008
792.8'2092—DC22
2007043798

The paper used in this publication meets the minimum requirements of American
National Standard for Information Sciences—Permanence of Paper for Printed Library
Materials, ANSI z39.48–1984. ∞

Cover image: Heinz teaching a master class at Kent State University, 1967.

All photographs appear courtesy of Barbara Schubert, unless otherwise noted.

Contents

Foreword

Heinz Poll has been a quiet major player in the rich history of international contributions to the creation of American dance, particularly American ballet. He worked outside the glittering parameters of New York City, once designated and probably still the dance capital of the world. But Heinz established rigorous standards for the art and its practitioners that have been felt and will be remembered far beyond the outer limits of Akron, the home base of his Ohio Ballet, as his touring dancers introduced audiences to a wide-ranging "library" of dance classics, all carefully chosen not only to educate and entertain audiences but also to develop well-rounded, more sophisticated performers.

The art of ballet in America has been shaped largely by men and women from other countries. Some stayed behind after tours of the United States, as early as the mid-eighteenth century, to set up studios and performing ensembles of their own. Some, like George Balanchine, sought a place where they could experiment freely with new ideas. And others, like Heinz Poll, made a conscious choice simply to throw in their lot with American dance in all its unruly, exasperating glory, whether as a teacher, choreographer, or company director.

Heinz was probably the earliest "crossover" ballet director, a man who drew his aesthetic naturally and equally from the German Expressionist modern-dance traditions of his youth and from formal ballet classicism. Productions of *The Nutcracker*, that holiday cash cow, were not for him, he would say firmly. Nor was he interested in reviving elaborate nineteenth-century ballet classics, he said, though in truth he did once collaborate on a staging of *The Sleeping Beauty* for another American troupe.

The repertory of Ohio Ballet was otherwise astonishingly eclectic and informed, including dances by twentieth-century masters like Paul Taylor, Merce Cunningham, and George Balanchine and individual classics like Antony Tudor's haunting *Dark Elegies*, a ballet portrait of a community mourning its lost children, and *Rooms*, Anna Sokolow's equally harrowing modern-dance depiction of the stark anomie of urban life.

Only the bigger, better-endowed Joffrey Ballet in New York had a comparable history of reviving little-known classics like Kurt Jooss's *Big City* and Ruthanna Boris's *Cakewalk*, both of which were signature ballets in the Ohio Ballet repertory. The scrupulously ballet-trained Ohio dancers took on the gymnastic oddities of Pilobolus's *Untitled*, another classic, and managed to look as comfortably accomplished in dances by postmodernists like Laura Dean, Lucinda Childs, and Molissa Fenley as they did performing ballet.

It is hard to imagine now, in the often blandly homogeneous ballet of the early twenty-first century, the thrill of seeing these dances side by side, along with Heinz's own classical choreography, which is sometimes luminous and sometimes chillingly sad and dark, but always flowing and musically adept. (Who but he would have had the curiosity and nerve to set a ballet about war to the limpid, lyrical piano pieces of Mendelssohn's *Songs without Words* and make it work against all expectations?)

The dancers Heinz worked with for thirty-one years at the Ohio Ballet, who eventually inherited his ballets, would probably have described him as a sternly demanding, uncompromising humanist. He believed in perfectability and often talked of acquiring pieces in these far-flung styles to develop his dancers. Like Balanchine, he believed in giving dancers what they could do but stretching that in nearly every dance. His company, founded with his life partner, Thomas Skelton, the brilliant and charming Broadway and dance lighting designer, was a microcosm of what dance and a dance company could be. It was not without faults, but the values that informed the company and what it danced made Ohio Ballet far more important than just a small, good troupe that survived and flourished for three decades in midwestern America.

And so the man himself is worthy of attention and study, in part because of his colorful life but even more because of how that life helped form this quiet, practical visionary of American dance. It is hard for me to write about Heinz as objectively, though, as I might. He is also wonderful company, as I discovered one gray February afternoon in 1986 when he walked into my life and took up residency there almost before I knew it.

The Ohio Ballet was about to open for a weeklong engagement at the Joyce Theater, an important dance space where the company was making its Manhattan debut. Heinz agreed to an interview that was to be done in the third-floor culture department at the *New York Times*, where I am a staff dance writer. I had warned him that I had a bad cold. If he wanted, we could certainly do the interview over the telephone. No, he said, he was not worried about catching my cold. And in he came, sitting down companionably and handing me a plastic delicatessen bag filled with fruit. Helpful, he assured me, for colds.

If I were putting together an album of choice memories, the first image would be of Heinz looking so at home in that uncongenial sea of dull gray metal desks as he withdrew green grapes from the bag. The photograph would be of a formal but pleasant-looking man, bespectacled, gray-haired, and a little roly-poly. He talked of what he looked for in dancers and of his ideas about technique and style, which were certainly unusual in a time when prodigious technical feats were becoming the apparent be-all and end-all of ballet, at least in New York City.

Fixed close to that first photograph would be an image of Heinz and Tom, whose sense of humor was even more wicked than Heinz's, in a raucous impromptu get-together sometime in the late 1980s, as I recall. The setting was the Here-U-R, a roadhouse where dancers hung out after performances, in Lee, Massachusetts, the next town over to the Jacob's Pillow Dance Festival, where Ohio Ballet was probably then performing.

There would be other snapshots on that page, of Heinz reveling in good food and conversation at a few favorite Manhattan restaurants. And perhaps there would be a photo he sent me of his beloved cat Benjamin, nestled next to a favorite catnip toy. And a few of the rambling farm that was a second home for him and Tom; Heinz delighted in the gnarled rock outcroppings and ruins, sunlit meadows, and interior mouse-nibbled living-room carpet.

On the next page would be a photographic portrait of a young ballerina who had performed briefly with the Ohio Ballet. She mentioned that experience to me in an interview, fastidiously wrinkling her delicate little nose. The company was fine. But Akron?

Ohio has a long, exceptionally strong tradition of homegrown dance. But my provincial New Yorker's fantasy of a place named Akron, which I've never visited, is of a smallish city with a lingering smell of coal in the air.

I look at an archival photo of Heinz rising from a huddle of dancers in a performance by the Chilean National Ballet in 1964. I think of his experiences in Berlin and of his love for the German Expressionist dancers whose work he admired, all the details of an unusual life recounted so vividly and so instructively in this memoir. I think of Heinz, a laid-back sophisticate with a gift for friendship, settling down in mid-America and making a new life for himself and for those around him.

If I turn the page then, in this imaginary album, I suddenly come upon a nameless young dancer soaring softly and voluptuously into midair in a perfectly shaped leap. She is a dancer I came upon in a ballet-school performance of *Giselle* in a drab high school auditorium in 1986. A banner year, it would seem. She danced Myrtha, the chill queen of the Wilis, the ghosts of women who die before marriage and who welcome the dead Giselle into their midst.

It was one of the most authoritative and nuanced Myrthas I had ever seen, performed though it was by a shortish, chubby seventeen-year-old girl with too-small feet that in the world of perfect bodies, a major criterion for a ballet career then and now, could only be described as spatulate. I longed to call a few friends who worked with ballet troupes and urge them to see her perform again that weekend. But there would have been no point.

A few years passed. Then, in a New York performance by Ohio Ballet, who but that young dancer should suddenly shoot across the stage. Heinz had seen past the imperfections to the artist beneath and had hired her. He wanted dancers with a strong but not necessarily perfect technique, he had told me in that 1986 interview. Size was not as important to him as personality, energy, and a hunger to bite into the ripe apple of a good dance.

"To me, an arabesque is an arabesque," Heinz told me then, in an observation that I believe helps define his life and vision and that certainly informs this rich memoir. "It can have many meanings. That is the choreography. An arabesque can have many textures. It can make the world stand still or make it tremble. And things have to make sense. You are not just writing lines to read between."

Jennifer Dunning

Editor's Preface

In 1972, I called the University of Akron for directions to the dance department, where I had been invited to watch a rehearsal of the Chamber Ballet and meet the directors, Heinz Poll and Thomas Skelton. Although I had lived in Cleveland most of my adult life, I had never ventured to Akron, only about thirty miles to the south. I had no idea then, or for several years after, that I would travel that road almost daily for nearly twenty years, working as volunteer, board member, general manager, and associate director of Ohio Ballet.

Among the greatest privileges of my life has been knowing and working with Tom Skelton and Heinz Poll. When Tom died of lung cancer in August 1994, we all knew that continuing to direct the Ohio Ballet would be a difficult challenge for Heinz. He met that challenge and continued to choreograph and direct his company until his retirement four years later. This was not a man who quit easily.

Heinz Poll was a fair person who never asked anything of anyone that he himself was unwilling to give. We once made a deal that he would not spend any money not specifically in the budget if I would not tell him how tight money actually was. We both kept our promises, and I believe that the miracle of Ohio Ballet's long and respected existence was in great part due to his focus on dance, rather than on expensive costumes and sets (Tom Skelton's fabulous lighting was created at almost no expense). Heinz created his dances with such a small budget that he often wanted the actual production cost to remain secret, lest the company be thought of in the dance world as less than truly professional.

Heinz Poll lived with one kidney his entire life and was advised to avoid any strenuous activity. Nevertheless, he continued to dance as long as he believed he looked good on the stage. He taught until he could no longer perform the lifts and turns he was asking his dancers to duplicate. He choreographed and directed the company he had founded with Tom Skelton until he believed the audiences were insufficient to support his work.

Perhaps to his own surprise, Heinz Poll enjoyed his retirement. He enjoyed the time to have lunch with friends and the opportunity to meet socially with dance critics and teachers with whom he had felt constrained while he was working. He loved having dinner at Severance Hall, home of the Cleveland Orchestra, before the concerts which he considered to be a glorious gift. He saw nine or ten productions at the Stratford Festival of Canada, in Ontario, each summer, and spent hours discussing them and marveling that he actually didn't dislike musicals as he had assumed he did. He liked watching my grandchildren (who called him Grandpa Heinz) grow, and he once commented that the eldest had perfect feet for a dancer. He fed the squirrels that gathered at his windowsills and the dogs and cats that ventured into his yard.

Heinz took the opportunity offered in retirement to work seriously on the manuscript of his memoir. He had learned English as a forty-year-old, when he came to the United States to live, and he retained his amusing grammatical and pronunciation errors all his life. When in Cleveland, he lived just across the driveway from our back door, in a guesthouse. He visited, almost daily, with a new batch of pages for me to read. We talked for hours about his experiences recorded in the memoir and of spelling and grammatical points, some of which he seemed not to take seriously. He never ceased to smile when I pointed out, once again, the difference between "know" and "no." In editing this book, I have attempted to be respectful of his style, except where it interfered with understanding.

Heinz's kidney began to fail in late 2005, and after several months of dialysis, during which he retained his sense of humor, he died in late April 2006.

Twelve years earlier, shortly before Tom Skelton's death in 1994, Tom wrote a note to Heinz that reads, in part, "You'll never be alone, HP, not with these glorious memories. Celebrate it." And we also celebrated, on July 21, 2006, when dancers, coworkers, and friends came to Cleveland from near and far to celebrate Heinz's life and to say, "We love you, and we miss you, Heinz."

I miss you, Heinz, and I especially miss the sound of your voice calling to me to read a letter from a beloved student or company member or a paragraph or chapter of this book. It helps, however, to know that your remarkable story and your best choreography will live on.

Heinz Poll's works have been archived at the University of Akron, which has made it possible for dance companies to revive them accurately. His choreography also continues to be performed annually in Akron at the Heinz Poll Dance Festival.

Barbara Schubert

Author's Preface

I wish to thank my friends John and Barbara Schubert for their invaluable encouragement and help in making this book possible. Their many hours spent reading and correcting a manuscript full of grammatical errors deserves my deepest appreciation. Thinking back about their many suggestions with the text, I know that I began to better understand the use and nuances of the English language. Thanks also to Jennifer Dunning, who many years ago urged me to complete an unfinished manuscript and who always followed its progress. Jennifer is the author of several books about dance, as well as a dance critic at the *New York Times*. Also thanks to Kathryn Karipides and Dennis Dooley for their generous comments.

A special thanks to my editors Michael Carley and Elton Glaser of the University of Akron Press for their patience and for pointing out to me the many sections in the manuscript that needed more complete information and clarification. Their contribution to the final version of the manuscript has been a special gift to me.

In 1971, I choreographed a ballet I named ... *a time to dance*, with music by Jefferson Airplane. America was at war, and the ballet suggested the parting of a young dancer from his girl, and finally his death at the end of the ballet. While searching for a title for the book, the name of the ballet came to my mind frequently. I finally chose A *Time to Dance* as the title, for no other reason than that it was an appropriate suggestion of the sequence of events in my life.

Everything I have written has come from recollections and memories of my family, the people I have met, and the things that happened in my life: from childhood and adolescence, from being a member of the German navy, to a student of dance, and from there to a career as dancer, choreographer, teacher, and ultimately, with Thomas Skelton, cofounder of Ohio Ballet and its artistic director. I always lived my life with passion and no regrets.

Heinz Poll

CHAPTER I

Youth

Recalling glimpses of my early childhood, I perceive a mosaic of events. There were the visits by St. Nikolaus, the patron saint of children, with his servant, Knecht Ruprecht. The highlight of those visits lay in my fearful anticipation of December 6. Any negative comments about my two older sisters or myself that had been communicated from my parents to the person responsible for impersonating the saint could result in severe admonishment by St. Nikolaus or physical punishment from his servant. Ruprecht, the carrier of presents and punishment, symbolized by a sack slung over his shoulder and a bunch of whisk-branches in one hand, always dressed in black and resembled a chimney sweeper, while St. Nikolaus was Santa, as we know him today. These visits were frightening to me as a child of four or five.

I remember the image of a streetcar depot across the street from the house where I was born on March 18, 1926, in the German city of Oberhausen im Rheinland. There were powerful rumblings every morning at exactly 6:00 when the huge doors of the depot would screech open to reveal the departing streetcars making their own earsplitting noise, a severe contrast to our usually quiet home.

I remember the sound of crackling chestnuts on our coal stove on many evenings during the cold of winter. The day when gaslight arrived in our humble dwelling proved a major event. And later, installment of a wall telephone brought with it considerable merriment. Mother had had a hard time figuring out which end of the phone belonged on the ear, which made her always speak into the receiver. Whenever she picked up the phone, we would all lie in wait to witness her switching the phone around.

Father's brothers, sisters, and parents lived in the same building, and all our dwellings were identical: a bedroom, a kitchen-living room, and, in our case, a small room behind a staircase where my sisters slept. I remember very little interaction between all those family members, perhaps because all of them dealt in the same business and product, fruits and vegetables.

At one point in 1932, the whole extended family split up, and Father moved us closer to the center of town. Here he was not far from his work, which had grown into a wholesale business. However, because of that growth, Mother had become part of the operation. By that time, I had entered public school, and I had begun to feel a kind of monotony in our daily life. But one day, through an unexpected action on my part, I discovered something new and worthy of note. While climbing the streetlamp across from our home, I experienced my first orgasm. I don't know if it could be called an orgasm, but I remember a powerfully tingling and pleasurable sensation in my groin. I could climb the lantern as often as I wished, in the process just beating my bent legs a couple of times, in order to achieve a state of momentary ecstasy without ejaculation.

Nothing in my recollection of that time seemed more important. Life offered little more than the changing of seasons. For some time, the streetlamp remained my best friend, until masturbation became the order of the day. No priestly intimidation would make me renounce those intimate moments. Every night I waited feverishly and impatiently for the house to be still so I could share my secret with myself.

Like most young boys in our neighborhood, I grew up in the typical bourgeois fashion with Mother, a staunch Roman Catholic, making sure I attended Mass on a regular basis after having entered public school at the age of six. My parents were hardworking people who had begun to establish their independence toward the end of the second decade of the twentieth century by buying fruits and vegetables from farms as far away as Hamm, a farming community near Düsseldorf, known to me as Kappes Hamm. (*Kappes* means cabbage in the regional dialect.) Father would leave home weekdays as early as 3:00 or 4:00 A.M., to return in his truck at about 7:00 A.M. from the farmers' auction house and sell whatever harvest had been available that day, at the market in Oberhausen.

The *Grossmarkt* (wholesale market) consisted of about eight wooden structures, each approximately the size of a barrack and large enough to hold the produce from a truckload, plus some more. One corner of the structure was converted into a tiny office where Mother collected the money, wrote the bills, kept the books, or, when business was slow, assembled local gossip for dinner-table conversation. This then was the place where Father, his brother Herman and his wife, and his sisters Gretchen and Änne, along with their husbands, ran their businesses, together with other merchants, peddling produce in bulk to the small businesses, who in turn carried the stuff two city blocks away to the public market. There the produce was sold by the piece or the pound directly to the consumer under those colorful little tent-roofs which so charmingly depict European quaintness on postcards.

The public market was also the center of Oberhausen im Rheinland, then a city of approximately 250,000 inhabitants. The market, a cobblestone area of about three hundred by three hundred feet, was surrounded by streets, through one of which a streetcar made its way. The buildings on the street behind the market housed one of the local newspapers and a restaurant. A major building on one side was home to the Berlitz School of Languages. All other buildings on this, the Gutenbergstrasse, were occupied by lawyers, dentists, and other professionals. To this day, the main artery of the city runs in front of the market with a newsstand on one corner, dominated by a large statue, the Germania, while right across the street stands the Herz Jesu Kirche. I still remember the smell of cold stone in semi-darkness inside the church, the remnants of burned-out incense and wax, and the smell of sweat the many sinners had left behind, similar to the smell in school, cold and acrid, accumulated over a century.

I remember Mother and Father coming home around 1:00 P.M. for lunch, the major meal of the day. Mother would empty a large leather pouch full of coins onto Father's desk, count the money, and figure there and then on the expense and the profit for the day. She carried into her old age the habit of rubbing her index and middle finger against her thumb.

Else, the younger of my two sisters, though nine years my senior, was in charge of the household and the cooking for the family. Änne, already twenty, proved to be useful in Father's business and, therefore, was excused from domestic chores. Inevitably, the conversation around the dinner table would center on the success of the day's business. Father's purchase that morning of the first carrots of the season would be touted as far superior to that of his sister and her no-good, much younger husband. The subject was spun into innumerable similar anecdotes about others. My presence would be acknowledged only when, after much shoptalk, the language would turn somewhat stronger, and here and there a word like "shit," accompanied by a whispered "sssssssssssht, the boy," would make me feel acknowledged as a member of the family.

Except for some occasional outings to the Ruhr in summertime with Mother and Aunt Emma (not my real aunt but Mother's best friend), I was pretty much left to myself. If Mother gave me something to remember her by, it would be her love of nature. She was a stout woman, capable of walking many miles, to and from Mühlheim an der Ruhr, where she and Father were born, through country and forests for hours on end. With her friend Emma beside her and engaged in nonstop gossip, we paused only once at a country inn for coffee and perhaps a piece of cake.

It must have been in 1933, when the Nazis had taken over, that Father became a member of the party. I was six years old at that time, and I assumed that everyone else belonged to the party. I didn't even know that to belong you had to join. Nothing of that particular period has left anything of importance in my memory. Hitler had come to power, but the significance of that event was lost not just on me, but on everyone else my age.

Father continued hoping that I, too, would one day sell carrots and cauliflowers in Oberhausen. He took me to his only diversions on Sundays, boxing or soccer. To his credit, I must say that he gave up on this part of my education graciously and after only two seasons. My father was a handsome man and often protective of me, whenever Mother, who employed a heavy hand when punishing, turned her anger on me for reasons I did not consider justified. However, Father and I never developed a father-son relationship. He was a gentle man, perhaps too shy to show emotion of any kind. He had another brother, Phillip, and a sister, Aunt Lieschen. Both were married but did not succeed in life. They worked for their well-to-do relatives whenever they were needed. Father always treated them with respect, and I remember their often cheerful presence in our home. They were my favorite relatives. Both had an exquisite sense of humor, as is often the case with people of little means. Their infectious laughter remains among the best memories of my childhood. Uncle Phillip had lost an eye, among a number of other wounds he had received during World War I. He sported a glass eye, which he would sometimes take out and deposit on top of the sandwich that was lying on a plate before me. One of my sisters would occasionally find his eye in her dish of pea soup. His joy at playing such innocent jokes on us was contagious, but we were always on the lookout whenever he appeared at our home. Aunt Lieschen had her own sense of humor, contained in a little book she always carried with her. She had written down close to three hundred jokes and numbered them. Father had only to ask that she tell us the story about the shipwreck again, and, without hesitation, she would declare under which number that story was to be found. Her visits were always punctuated by someone asking for one of her stories, and, with a twinkle in her eyes, she always obliged.

Sister Else, the family's Cinderella by choice or necessity, a fact I will never know the truth about, did, in the end, marry Prince Charming. If not the prince of fairy tales, he nonetheless was endowed with a beautiful physique, blue eyes, blond hair, and a big heart. Josef and Else had been childhood friends, and, for as long as I can remember, he worked for Father. The air was always laden with sensuous flirtation when he was around. He was a real heartthrob with the ladies. They eventually had a daughter, Gisela, in 1942.

In 1934, Father decided that Änne should open her own business on the public market, starting by selling potatoes. It was there in the market, selling potatoes under her little colorless tent on the far end of the plaza, that Änne met Leo. She and Leo, who had been a sailor on the battleship *Köln*, fell in love, and soon they sold potatoes side by side. I never learned Leo's last name, and he remained forever just Leo who was liked by the whole family. He was a sunny, easygoing fellow, and I adored him because he insisted on taking me along when they spent their weekends in a tent-community along the Ruhr, where everybody rowed in kayaks. We took long trips, and I loved to paddle away at my own leisure while Änne and Leo would sunbathe in the back. I was eight years old when

Leo convinced my parents that my desire to roller-skate and ice-skate were perfectly normal for a boy. I had wanted roller skates for years, confiding my wish only to Else, who warned me that asking for them would surely mean disappointment. But in 1934, on entering our living room on Christmas morning, I laid eyes on my first pair of roller skates. I knew it was Leo whom I had to thank.

Christmas day will stay forever etched in my mind as a time of love and giving. Mother, Father, Änne, and Else had worked all day, the day before Christmas, selling Christmas trees on a street corner downtown. After supper that evening, my sister Else and I were sent to bed while Father and Mother would spend most of the night dressing our tree (we burned real candles then), arranging the presents, always unwrapped, and plates heaped with fruits, nuts, sweets, homemade cookies, and chocolates. On Christmas mornings around 6:00 A.M., the smell of freshly ground and brewed coffee, plus Father's heavenly cigars, made those days always very special. We all felt excited and festive. During breakfast in our kitchen, I could hardly sit still. All I could think of was the moment when Father would open the door to the living room with the lighted tree in sight and where the overwhelming smell of cinnamon, nutmeg, oranges, and apples filled the air. We children made our own gifts. My sisters had remade old worn-out knitwear into new sweaters, scarves, mittens, and hats. Old clothing, also reshaped, shortened, or lengthened, dyed, or all of the above, became unrecognizable in its new state. Only the gifts Father and Mother gave were truly new. I had made boxes out of cartons, wood, and even pieces of old rugs. Everything was glued, painted, and filled with everybody's favorite sweets; they made wonderful presents. After gift-giving, we would all sit down, sated with joy, and sing "Silent Night" and "O Tannenbaum," in that order. Father, whom I knew mostly as a hardworking man who seldom addressed me and whose honest and serious ways we all respected, suddenly sang so loud, as if he had taken lessons for the occasion. I always watched him spellbound because of the candles reflecting in his eyes. I sensed that, under that stern façade he displayed on a daily basis, perhaps another, warmer person lay dormant. My wish about that possibility was the reason I would break out in tears every time at that particular moment. However, I do not remember ever having heard the words "I love you" (*Ich liebe dich* in German). Sentiments were simply not expressed. Duty, obedience, and discipline were our leitmotif. The happy times I have described were always determined by events dictated exclusively by the dates on calendars and followed religiously. That's the way I grew up.

Mother, with Aunt Emma, took to making a yearly pilgrimage to the city of Kevelaer, perhaps a few hours by train from our hometown. Kevelaer played home every year to a large population of Catholics from the Rhein-Ruhr region who attended the symbolic reenactment of Christ carrying his cross. Mother could not resist buying little bottles, supposedly containing authentic splinters from the cross. Everywhere people seemed exalted, praying and singing with such fervor that it affected all. Church bells always rang, demanding that we kneel and pray. Mother bought me, in miniature, everything priests use to celebrate Mass, including a tabernacle with an imitation sacred host. As I was never allowed to ask any questions, her unusual generosity made me suspect that maybe it would please her if I should become a priest when I grew up.

Dear Mother, whatever you wanted me to be, I will never know. We were like strangers, always afraid of telling any truth about any-

thing we really felt. How much I would have liked to confide in you! Instead I had to take my love and secrets to strangers who, in turn, became mothers, fathers, and friends to me. But none of them were you, and I suspect I would have made you happier, would you have let me. I thank you for buying me those trinkets because they played an important role in my understanding of myself. You see, I closed the door to my room and, complete with bed sheet around my shoulders and my own altar, I held Mass. Without knowing it, you gave me my first real opportunity in life: I ACTED.

CHAPTER 2
1934–39

The house in which Father rented the second floor belonged to a butcher. His store was, and still is, on street level, beneath what used to be my parents' bedroom. He was not an ordinary butcher, but one who dealt exclusively in horsemeat and its by-products, like ground meat, cold cuts, and sausages. Through his shop window, one could detect enormous carcasses of meat hanging from the ceiling. I entered this store perhaps once or twice during our almost four-year tenancy, mainly because I must have harbored some sort of morbid curiosity.

Streets were still made of cobblestones, and ours, the Styrumer Strasse, somewhat narrow and not very long, crossed over the main artery of town one block to our right. Across the street from us, a small lane approximately 150 feet in length led to the Friederich-Karl Strasse with a short shopping strip that, if one turned left, led to the post office across from the old train station. On the corner across from us, a small family-run grocery store sold pickled cabbage and herring straight from the barrels, and everything else needed for daily consumption. There was a time when a cup of the foul-smelling juice from the herring barrel saved my life. While I was bedridden with infected swollen tonsils, Mother took the salty brew from an open barrel and poured it into my mouth. The salt opened the swollen gland immediately, thus returning to normal color my already blue face.

Adjacent to the food store were several small one-family houses. The family in the house closest and practically across from us had two children my age, a boy and a girl. We used to walk to and from school together, and sometimes Mother gave permission for me to stay at their home for supper, after we had collectively dealt with homework. We were different from most of the bullying crowd in our school, the *Marktschule*. Aggressive, vulgar, and loud, they made school an unpleasant experience for me. The best time of the day was when I could leave behind school and its stale stench of farts, puberty, and chalk.

There were other reasons why school did not appeal to me. I quickly had developed a mistrust of my teachers because they disapproved if anyone questioned their personal interpretation of every word in a book. My habit of trying to find different explanations for seemingly established fact made me extremely unpopular, and a number of students, encouraged by the teachers, made fun of me, which made me withdraw from all extracurricular activities. Since I was always inclined to spend my time alone, the events at school made me withdraw even more, and I became a loner. At home my behavior was interpreted as capricious, antisocial, and, worst of all, lazy; my parents wondered out loud who of our ancestors would have to be blamed.

Sex, or the mention of it, was absolutely taboo, and even my older sisters found it perfectly proper to keep me in the dark about the difference between boys and girls. Having discovered the secret quite some time earlier, when cousin Otto and I had engaged in mutual masturbation and he told me all there was to know, I took it as a challenge to play innocence incarnate. Cousin Otto was two years older than I and professed to know it all through his association with an older woman. The older woman, a friend of a female cousin of ours, turned out to be twelve years of age.

The year before my first communion was to take place, Mother stepped up her hidden desire to push me toward sainthood. From now on, it was daily attendance at Mass, before school and without breakfast, until communion had been received. I was to be kept pure in spirit and soul and did my best not to disrupt the harmony of our family routine. Clouds began to form the day Mother took me to a department store to purchase the inevitable communion suit. I was shattered when she adamantly refused my wish for a suit that would signal the end of childhood, namely a suit with long trousers. Most of the boys who received communion with me already wore long trousers. There and then I stopped being Mother's boy; I pouted and cried in front of the sales personnel, which infuriated her. Father, I guess, would have sided with me, but he had no say in such matters. It had always been an unspoken truth that Mother alone was in charge of my upbringing.

When the great day arrived, Father and my sisters were having breakfast in the kitchen, while Mother and I were at war in my room. She still insisted on dressing me, first the long black woolen stockings held by a rubber band and buttoned on to a sort of garter belt. I dared to voice my displeasure at the horrible itch those woolens produced, which elicited a slap in my face. Mother tensed, her eyes hardened like gray marbles, and her look shattered any hope of forgiveness for the rest of the day; I knew Mother. We stood wordless while she watched me dress myself the rest of the way: white shirt with bow tie, the short ugly pants and jacket made of wool jersey, and finally the cap with a cross attached in front. White lace handkerchief and prayer book in one hand, the other firmly in her grip, I walked with her the four blocks to our church; or better, she marched and I was pulled along, with Änne and Else behind. An assortment of family and friends waiting outside the church expressed admiration for my appearance and Mother's impeccable taste. We all took to our pews. I do not recall Father being present. He was an Evangelist, an arm of the Protestant Church and, as I found out much later, had stopped going to religious services after returning from World War I.

Standing in line, waiting for my turn in the confessional, I began to speculate on why it took some of the boys so long to reemerge from the booth. After confession the day before, how many sins could they have committed? But perhaps they confessed not just the act but every thought about sex, which would explain the delay.

Finally, assembled in the back of the church, final instructions whispered, burning candle in one hand and prayer book in the other, we made our way, in a procession, to the front. Halfway down the aisle, a feeling of relief from the pull of the rubber band on my upper left leg told me that something was going awfully wrong. Only two pews away, Mother was sitting erect and proud like a hen after having laid that perfect egg. I slouched forward, dragging my leg so as not to move it much out of fear for the worst, while holding candle and book. Just as I passed her, my stocking began to slide. I agonized under Mother's unbelieving stare at my appearance. Reaching the front of the church, with one leg bare for the whole world to see and trembling while kneeling down, I thrust my red face, with tongue sticking out, at the priest. I got up with my head bowed, trying to mingle as best as I could with the other boys, and made my way back to Mother's pew. Not looking at me, but moving her lips in wordless prayer, she blew out the candle and placed it on the floor. My hands my own again, I pulled up my stocking and fastened it with a safety pin she had taken from her purse. We sat, it seemed, the longest time. Mother had resumed her wordless prayer, and I, still numb, tried to imagine what lay ahead of me for the rest of the day.

When the Mass was over and everyone was filing out, I spotted Leo and Änne in conversation on the street. She was obviously giving him a shorthand description of my unfortunate mishap. Waiting for a sign of Leo's reaction, I noticed the smile that crept over his face. Given his nature, he obviously could picture the funny side of the situation. Soon a good number of relatives, including, of course, Aunt Emma, had assembled. With everyone pretending that nothing out of the ordinary had occurred, we all walked to our home.

Father must have spent a considerable amount of money, because the reception held in our tiny living room seemed to me lavish by our standards. The reason for this feast vanished soon after a certain amount of schnapps and beer had washed away restraint and churchly behavior. Stories, accompanied by much laughter, turned bawdy and louder by the minute, to be interrupted only by the priest's visit. For fifteen minutes, with already sheepish smiles and glassy eyes, everybody pretended to listen to his stories. Finally, after having eaten his piece of cake and after blessing the room, the food, and us, he left. I was sure that before reaching the street he must have thought he heard what sounded like the whooshing of bottles being opened.

After a couple of hours, which had included sister Else's rendering of an aria from the operetta *Der Tzarewitch*, Mother, and everyone else it seemed, had forgotten that I was around. By the way things looked, it was obvious that the party would go on until late. At last, Leo intervened in my favor, asking permission for me to change clothes for my favorite activity, roller-skating. A short time before, one corner of the public market had been paved and converted into a skating area. Some older children and some young adults had acquired considerable skill at skating, and I secretly wished to be included in what seemed to be a very privileged sensation of floating freely and effortlessly along. Eventually, I, too, became a capable skater. Later, at fourteen, when I had expanded that skill to the ice, I won a regional championship. The mention of my name in the paper gave me at last legitimacy as a normal boy. Had I won that prize playing soccer, it would have made me a hero in town, but getting some respectful looks from the older guys in school taught me very early about the power of the press.

Around that time, our class, in its single cultural excursion, ended up in the local theater to see a play. In searching my memory for any clues as to what we saw, my recollection stops right here. All I remember is the notion that something extraordinary had come over me when we had entered the theater. A sense of emotional thrill told me that this was my church, where I wished to and must worship. From then on, I lived in a kind of euphoria, never missing a day without passing the façade of the theater, which stood on a corner, separated by a street from a small park that later became the city's official outdoor roller-skating rink. My newfound passion at times gave way to acute despair. Not knowing how to deal with such contradictory emotions, I began to feel real pain. How could I understand and communicate to another person a state of being that had no source of reference or resolution? What was it I wanted to do in this place anyhow? It must have been the goings-on on the stage and not just this mysteriously darkened space that had caught my imagination. To be sure, the richly decorated theater, all red velvet, white walls, and golden ornamentation, the smell, the air, and the suspense, all played an important part in this moment of extraordinary attraction. It became clear to me that to be one of the people who inhabited the stage, I had to become someone who could in some capacity participate in its activities. In the end, I settled for acting, which meant that I had to learn it from someone.

Of course, there was no way to communicate a wish so crazy and daring to my parents and sisters, or even to Leo, whom I trusted most. And for the longest time I carried the truth about my decision to become an actor some day as a secret, until such time as one member of the family asked me the question (and because the conversation centered around my reputation as a useless dreamer), "What are you going to do with your life?" It must have been fear that the question would never be asked again. My answer came spontaneously and without the slightest delay. "I AM GOING TO BE AN ACTOR."

My answer elicited a chorus of laughter, accompanied by a few mocking and snide remarks from my older sister. Deeply hurt by my family's reaction, I retreated to my room in the attic, having lost all confidence of ever being able to communicate with any member of the family.

Who would argue that absolute loneliness of spirit could scar the soul forever? Yes, most will regain confidence and even profit in areas where the intellect triumphs over the truth. But what about the ones who carry their wounds like tattoos, never to be erased?

Both of my parents had been born into poverty. About Mother's family I do not know very much, remembering only having met her two half-brothers and especially a half-sister, Aunt Klara. When I was a very young child, my maternal grandmother would sometimes be in charge of me for an afternoon in her very small two-room dwelling where Mother had been born. The story of my grandmother carrying me in one arm and defending a small vessel of milk on her stove from a hungry rat with a red-hot poker has stayed engraved in my mind as the only picture of my grandmother.

My grandfather on Father's side sold potatoes at the local market. As young boys and teenagers, Father and his brothers worked for him. In later years, my cousins and I would at times witness his violent mood swings, caused by his excessive consumption of alcohol. Father and his brothers were often called upon to defend their mother from being beaten and otherwise abused by him. Alcohol ultimately caused his death, and while the adult family members sat gathered around my grieving grandmother in one room, my cousins and I entertained ourselves pulling the dead man's chest hair to be assured of his demise, while he was lying displayed in his casket in the only other room.

I remember Mother telling me, in 1946, after I had entered the dance division of the *Folkwangschule* in Essen-Werden, about her Saturday night's diversions, where she and Father had danced the nights away and won a ballroom dancing contest. They had met on one of those nights and married in 1913 when both were twenty years of age. Three months later my oldest sister Änne was born. Separation during the First World War brought much hardship for Mother, but after the war was over and Father had returned unharmed, they set out to make the best out of life. At first they both worked selling potatoes at the market, until, through determination and hard work, they became the owners of a retail business for fruits and vegetables.

By 1936, things were going well for the family. Father's business prospered. Änne and Leo had been engaged the previous year, while Else spent her weekends now with friends, getting tanned in summer or going out to dances during the winter months. Father, Änne, and Leo attended the 1936 Olympic games in Berlin for a week. That was Father's first vacation ever, while Mother continued her excursions with Aunt Emma, but mostly now without me.

At some time I had become a member of the Hitler Youth, not by choice, but because it had become a must. The nature of such organizations meant singing and marching together, it meant soccer and boxing—in short, everything I hated to do—and those hours became loathsome. At swimming pools I found myself being pushed into the water. My shins and nose got the worse of it from trying to play soccer and defending myself at boxing sessions. I hated those outings. When we had to stay overnight in tents, I burned myself attempting to make a campfire, got stung by three bees simultaneously, and had to defend myself from bad-smelling guys who in the dark of night tried to become intimate.

On the positive side, my roller- and ice-skating had improved considerably, which made me somewhat popular within that special fraternity. It was always my sister Else who took me to a park with a small lake during the winter months. There we would skate together until very late with many other aficionados and Else's male friends. The most beautiful, haunting hours were after dark, when gas lanterns illuminated the area, and barrels filled with glowing charcoal gave warmth after too much exposure to the icy air. Winters were very cold then. Once I saw the Rhein so frozen that trucks and cars ignored the bridges, making their way across wherever there was a point of access.

I still shared the walks to and from school with my two friends from across the street, but something had come between us. For one thing, I noticed the absence of invitations to spend time together, even to do homework. I blamed much of it on the fact that I, too, had changed. A boy at school whose sensibilities and disposition were very much in tune with mine had become my friend. Also cousin Otto, who visited more frequently and whose desire for masturbation sessions had increased, monopolized part of my free time.

One morning as I entered the kitchen, I saw the door to the hall open. At the end, Mother stood by the window looking at the street below, and, as I approached, I noticed that she was crying. It seemed to me that people were led away on the street. The men who led them wore civilian clothes, and their self-assured way of walking made it clear that they were in charge. In the distance, I spotted my two friends from across the street with their parents. All the people carried suitcases.

Mother, where are they going?

To America, they are being sent to America, this is where they want to go.

Why, Mother?

They are Jews.

What are Jews, Mother?

Don't ask so many questions, boy. One day you will understand.

I had become aware of the word "Jews" while listening to speeches on the radio by either Hitler or Göbbels. The family would always listen with grave expressions, and I would try to read their faces. Hitler's voice sounded always so loud and distorted that I was unable to understand him at all. Words like DEUTSCHLAND, EIN VOLK, JUDEN, and FEINDE became memorable because they were repeated with such frequency that they became the basic leitmotif to which people reacted, shouting HEIL in extraordinary unison.

One Sunday, Hitler was expected to speak to us, the Hitler Youth, at a large rally somewhere in one of the neighboring cities. We were herded by the thousands, starting at 6:00 A.M., to an open field. I had never seen so many of us at once. There was something frightening about the sense of loneliness among so many. We hardly spoke to each other, and a collective fear of isolation came over us, as we were grouped into blocks and blocks of youth in brown shirts.

It was summer, and we were facing the rising sun, waiting for Hitler to arrive, when a slight urge to urinate made me wonder how long I could hold out before having to ask permission to go. But to go where? As far as I could see, there were only kids in brown shirts and no place in sight where anyone could relieve himself. On this treeless field with only a Red Cross ambulance five or six blocks away, hope vanished and desire increased rapidly once I realized the horror of my situation. Simply wetting my pants was not the answer as they were short, and the trickle of urine down my legs and on my shoes would be the epitome of embarrassment. I held, and finally fainted, wetting myself after all. I woke up in the ambulance, where I had been held for an hour or so before being returned to my unit. Soon after, we left. Hitler never came.

Deliberately skipping Sunday school and using the donation money, I saw my first movie: *Rose Marie*, with Jeanette MacDonald and Nelson Eddy. Someone close to the family had seen me and reported to Mother. After I got a good beating from her, Father declared that I should be given some pocket money on Sundays to use as I liked. This marked the first time Father had intervened in my behalf, and after that Sundays became movie days. Among many, one of my favorites was Laurel and Hardy (*Dick und Doof* in German, translated as "Fat and Stupid"). My love for the theater had never lessened, and although tickets were inexpensive, it was not the price that kept me from going but my short pants, which prevented my admission without an adult.

Around the time that Father began giving me pocket money for movies, he bought a new truck and a house. With business seemingly in excellent shape and the population gradually recovering from shortages of food, goods, and money, Father bought a little house in the suburb of Alstaden, with a loan for down payment from Mother's half-brother, Uncle Gottfried. Only a thirty-minute walk from downtown Oberhausen, the suburb was home to many Polish immigrants. The nearby towers of the coal mines spread their somber shadows over the area, and two blocks away, a crematorium for dead animals sent its terrifying stench our way whenever the wind blew in our direction.

The small house was L-shaped. Else and I shared two tiny attic rooms above Father and Mother's bedroom. A living room, Änne's room, a kitchen barely large enough to accommodate a coal stove, a pantry, a table and some chairs, and an adjoining laundry room completed the living quarters. An outhouse was attached to the wall of the laundry room from the outside, and a shed stood nearby, where tools, ropes, and empty fruit crates were stored. Approximately one-half acre of land was part of the property, surrounded by other homes and little gardens. All buildings were the color of soot, and the soil, practically black, had to be heavily fertilized every spring, which was a sort of communal ritual. By mutual agreement, all neighbors carefully deposited the contents of their outhouses on the garden soil, usually a week before planting time. By late summer, I found myself bedridden with jaundice for the duration of six weeks. Having to live exclusively on water crackers and tea, I survived, and with assurances of permanent immunity.

The new Catholic school I attended was much less rowdy, and my teachers were more sympathetic and accepting of me. Every morning before classes began, we prayed. One morning, our teacher announced that prayers in schools had been forbidden by the authorities. He then went ahead and prayed anyway, with all of us joining in. That was the last class he gave to us; we never saw him again. Soon after, for reasons unknown to me, I was sent to a different school only three or four blocks away.

During weekends in fall and winter, I would take the train to Essen, which had the only indoor ice-skating rink, in order to practice. It was my assigned trainer who encouraged me to take ballet lessons in order to improve my line. I did not know what ballet meant or was, but he nevertheless gave me the address of a school in my hometown. It turned out that a woman who also set the dances for operas and operettas in the theater ran the school. Thanks to her position, I was finally able to attend several rehearsals of the theatrical performances she had been involved with. Whenever possible, I would help Änne and Leo with minor chores at the market, thus being able to augment my pocket money for the lessons. Classes consisted mainly of stretching and following her moves to the strains of Strauss waltzes, usually the same ones. The procedure struck me as somewhat ridiculous, perhaps because I was the only boy in attendance, but her influence in making it possible for me to set foot in the theater made me continue. My visits to that school remained forever unknown to the family, since I made sure not to be seen entering and leaving the building, which was in a remote part of the city. It was presumed that I would outgrow any notion of pursuing anything but Father's business.

I loved ice-skating! What a joy to feel the absolute absence of gravity, the closest I would ever come to flying free, like a bird. I still remember the clumsiness I experienced when I had to change from skates to shoes; my body weight seemed to triple.

In 1939, when the war broke out, I remember one of our neighbors coming over to give the news to Mother who, besides me, was the only one at home. She had heard about it on the radio, and both women cried bitterly. Both had experienced World War I, and they anticipated the consequences of another war. They soon set out to visit the closest food store in hopes of stocking up on whatever would still be available, but they ended up with just a few bars of soap. When Father got home, we assembled in front of our radio, listening to snippets of news about the invasion of Poland and assurances that victory was expected in no time at all. At age thirteen, I didn't read newspapers and, therefore, had no knowledge of any differences between Germany and Poland, or any other country for that matter. Ears and eyes alert, I tried to read everybody's thoughts, reactions, and expressions, to learn more about what was going on. From the looks on their faces, it became clear to me that something inevitably gloomy had taken place. My romantic notion of war being mysterious and adventurous soon faded after listening to speech after speech on the radio, all of them accusing and full of anti-Polish slogans. Much later I realized that I had witnessed the signs that were to change the Germany of my innocent childhood. To me, the rest of the world, like all of us, went to church on Sundays and worked on weekdays, and children went to school and obeyed.

In 1940, an event occurred that would deeply and for a long time affect my relationship with my family. It turned out that Leo was half Jewish. His mother was a Jew, while his father, an Aryan who held an important position at a local police department, made sure that the family's identity was kept a secret. I had met them once, including Leo's brother Kurt, when my family had spent New Year's Eve at their home in 1936. But now a confrontation had taken place between Father, Änne, and Leo, who supposedly had asked Änne to go with him to nearby Holland to get married. Apparently, after learning just then about Leo's status as a non-Aryan, which would make marriage for them impossible in the Third Reich, Father threw a fit. I witnessed his anger at Änne. He took all her belongings and threw them out onto the street for all the neighbors to see and asked her to leave his house. Änne left! I was inconsolable. Turning in my grief to Mother and Else, I was told that there was nothing to do; after all, Leo was a Jew.

In 1980, Änne, on a visit to the U.S., confessed to me that the family had staged this confrontation to confuse the neighbors, who apparently had gotten wind about the fact that Leo was not an Aryan. Out of fear that I, in innocence, could spill the beans, I was made a witness but kept in the dark about the truth. Änne and Leo never married. Leo had gone so far as to ask about an audience with Göbbels. After all, he had served for many years on the Panzerkreutzer Köln. *The audience was refused.*

Because of my profound dislike of all activities during the meetings at the house of the Hitler Youth, I had skipped a number of visits. When someone appeared at our home to report my absences, Father, without saying a word, walked to our shed where I kept my skates and destroyed them in one blow, making sure that in so doing he was seen by the boy who had been sent to our home. I was in absolute shock. How could Father, who had never raised a hand against me, do such a thing? There would remain so many unanswered questions about certain attitudes my family displayed at this time, attitudes that seemed to be based on fears. When I carefully listened to some of their conversations, I could detect a hint of more carefully articulated wording, so different from the times before the war when everything about life seemed to be fun.

Father's drastic reaction to my having missed several meetings with the Hitler Youth had met with Mother's and Else's approval, and communication between us came to a complete standstill. We avoided looking at each other and ate our meals with only the ticking of the kitchen clock and the sound of spoons and forks on plates as conversation.

After what seemed ages to me, I finally learned from Else that Änne was working as a waitress somewhere in a Swiss border town, which ultimately turned out to be the city of Köln, after an admission made later by Änne. It was obvious that my sisters exchanged mail through a third party, who turned out to be Leo's mother. Through her, it was also revealed to us that Leo had volunteered and been drafted into the *Arbeitsdienst,* a labor force known as the Organisa-

tion Todd. This organization, administered by Fritz Todd, the builder
of the Autobahn, was in charge of construction and highway defense.
The men in this unit, mostly political foes and other undesirables,
were treated like slave labor. As a half Jew, Leo could not serve in the
German army, but to show that he was a committed German, he had
volunteered and been sent to the south of France after that country's
invasion in 1940 by the German army, to work on the construction
of what was then known as the West Wall. When the construction
of the wall neared its completion, Leo had been assigned the task of
deactivating the Allied bombs that had failed to explode on impact.
We called them *Blindgänger*, and Leo died when one of the bombs
exploded on him. It was Leo's mother who had been informed about
the accident, and it was she who contacted Änne and directed her
to the city where Leo was dying. Unfortunately, Änne did not reach
him before he died.

Thinking back on those times, I realize I was living in a vacuum, without any sense of time or permanence. News about my
sister Änne was all that could bring a flicker of excitement into
an otherwise dull and colorless existence. It was a gray and rainy
day when Else announced to me that, on the following Sunday, we
were to visit with Änne at the ice-skating rink in Essen. Änne was
coming especially to visit with me. When we did meet, I only cried
and held on to her for the longest time. That was, after all, the first
time I had missed someone I knew and loved, and I was determined
not to let her go again. I do not know if it was actually I who convinced them both that Änne should come home with us that same
afternoon. Änne's sudden willingness to do so, after such a dramatic departure several months before, gave rise to my suspicion
that the whole charade had perhaps been prearranged by Mother
and Else, and maybe Father, too. All I had been told was that only
Mother knew about our meeting in Essen. After a short phone con-

versation had taken place between Else and Mother, I was advised that the visit at home had to be cut short, so as to be over before Father's return from his soccer game.

Änne's reunion with Mother was nothing short of emotional, in a sort of Anglo-Saxon way, and her need to depart before Father's arrival was simply and unexplainably overlooked. When he finally entered our living room he didn't seem overly surprised. They both just gravely nodded their heads, saying *Guten Tag, Vater* and *Guten Tag, Änne* to each other. Shortly thereafter, Änne became again part of the family routine.

CHAPTER 3
The War Years

Josef, Else's husband, had been drafted when the war broke out, and now, in 1941 at the age of forty-eight, it was Father's turn. I can still see him assembling his shaving utensils on the morning of his departure. Only Mother and I were present, and it all seemed strangely eerie. The tone of his voice had dropped an octave, and Mother spoke softly. I was unable to make out what they were saying to each other as both were speaking in their peculiar dialect, something that turned their conversation always into a private affair. At this time, Änne and Else were working in the *Warnzentrale*, located in the basement of the post office in Oberhausen, a place in charge of warning the large war industry in the Ruhr area of approaching bomber squadrons from the west.

With Father gone to war, the business closed, and with the increasing frequency of bombardments, the grim reality of war made itself felt. It was a time when it was futile to sleep without our clothes on. A small suitcase with just essentials was always kept in our tiny basement, where we took refuge as soon as the sirens howled their warning. On one of those nights, Änne and I, after about twenty minutes in confinement, decided to go outside. We could hear the planes and the faint explosions of bombs in the distance, but agreed that the fact that "they are not over us" would give us a chance to witness that strange turbulence in the sky, the sounds of which had become so familiar.

The night was light and clear, and I remember a cloudless sky with not a star missing. The explosions produced by the flak (anti-aircraft artillery) seemed like miniature fireworks. We watched fascinated, until we saw a little plane, high up in the air and barely visible, swooping up and down in circles trying to escape the flak, an image I will always remember.

Several months passed by. Our only occupation consisted of safeguarding ourselves from the ever-increasing attacks from above and making sure that Mother would be able to prepare one hot meal a day, usually one kind of root vegetable cooked with potatoes or sugar beets and mashed together. To that purpose, we had, like all our neighbors, a small but richly outhouse-fertilized vegetable garden behind the house, but it took considerable skill to keep the thieves away at night. Finally, our dog Fanny, who hated to spend the nights outside, became the protector of the garden because of her powerful bark. It was an unspoken truth by now that people kept their pets inside by day and night for fear that they may turn up as stews on somebody's dining table. Fanny was vicious and loud around strangers, and she survived. Stealing from gardens and trees became a sort of sport for years to come and even lasted for several years after the war had ended. Major damage usually occurred when people had to spend time in bunkers or basements, leaving their gardens without protection.

I took part in many such excursions and must have been very good at it because I was never caught. The loot consisted basically of apples in the fall, sugar beets and turnips in the winter, and whatever was available during the spring and summer months. Often two thieves would simultaneously prowl the same territory, scare each other away, and leave the goods to a third party. It became a sort of entertainment, often the only one to look forward to, for young and old. It reached its high point in August when the first tomatoes, plump and red, had to be protected behind rows of barbed wire and similar contraptions. People usually planted them below their open bedroom windows and had developed a kind of special sensitiv-ity about approaching thieves, rather like the handicapped, whose deafness or blindness forces them to acquire different resources for sensing oncoming danger.

Austria's *Anschluss* (annexation) to the Reich in 1938 had pre-ceded the invasion of Poland in 1939, to be followed in 1940 with the occupation of France, Belgium, Holland, and other countries to the east. It all culminated with Hitler's invasion of the USSR in 1941. The Second World War had escalated to far more than just the promised blitzkrieg of two years before. It also meant that all of my childhood dreams were being pushed into an uncertain future. There was little else in the world that could arouse my interest but my love of skating and the theater. When I was listening to clas-sical music on the radio, which my family termed "heavy music," my focus would sometimes shift from acting to perhaps playing an instrument, anything that would permit my access to the stage.

Before Father left, he had once taken me with him to Köln, where he attended a major auction. He left me to explore the city by myself. It was an early afternoon, and on impulse I decided to attend a concert at a hall not far from our point of departure. The immediacy of the live orchestra produced its magic; I sat rapt, lis-tening to what I would discover later had been Brahms's Second Piano Concerto. In the midst of the first movement, the howling of sirens announced approaching enemy planes. Musicians and audience rose with surprising calm, making their way to the bun-ker located under the theater. After a tense forty-five minutes, the sirens once again sounded, but this time with much less urgency to my ears. When we had emerged from the depths and with reassurances from the management that only a few firebombs had fallen in some part of the city, an offer was made to reimburse those who felt compelled to leave. The musicians and most of the audience once more took to their seats, and the concert continued, beginning this time with the second movement of the concerto.

A high school education seemed superfluous in our working class family. All I needed to learn were certain skills to run Father's business. All my cousins were expected to follow the route my uncles and aunts had taken, and all of them did. In 1940, after I had graduated from public school at the age of fourteen, I spent one unsuccessful year at the *Höhere Handelsschule* (Business High School), with rock-bottom grades, before working as an office apprentice for the Kork and Kieselgur Werke Kempchen, until age sixteen. After almost ten months, my attempt at office work had failed dismally. The owner of the firm that produced cork, and a pebbly substance called Kieselgur, labeled me a dreamer. With no visible future for myself, and anticipating the inevitable fact of being drafted very soon, I announced at age seventeen that I wished to volunteer my service in the army. It was 1943, and I had felt a depressing sense of boredom. The daily and nightly routine, going to and from home to the bunker a couple of blocks away, plus the lack of any stimulus, especially any meaningful communication with anyone my age, made me want to experience a complete change in life. My sister Änne was able to pull some strings with friends who worked at the local draft board to make the navy my call of duty. Since the navy was considered to be the least offensive of the armed forces, it was made clear to me that I was among the privileged few to be included in this service at this stage of the war. I had always considered the navy's uniform its most attractive selling point.

After Father and sisters had said their good-byes to me, Mother and I stood at the platform of the train station, saying all the things mothers and sons say on such occasions, when the future seems unknown. We cried a little, while I listened to her last-minute advice on the dangers and consequences associated with encounters of the opposite sex. After that we remained silent. When the train had finally departed, she grew smaller and smaller in proportion to my growing anguish of losing her from sight. And then she was gone.

But I was not ready yet to look at what lay ahead of me. The immediate past had left too many questions unanswered. The banishing of Änne from our home, and the subject of Jews, and my parents' real view of it all had never come up again after Änne's return home. There was too much to come to terms with. I had been extremely sensitive to the fact that, for the first time in my life, my family had suddenly treated me, after I had voiced my decision to enlist, as something special. A gleam in their eyes had made that sense of pride and awe unequivocal, and it left me confused as to my real worth to them. Was my mother proud, like many mothers at the time, that her son was offering his life to the Führer? At least that was what the propaganda machine made us believe. After all, mothers whose sons got killed in the war were decorated for sacrificing their offspring. The answer, of course, would have been pure speculation, but the times were ripe for harboring suspicions, encouraged through every devious means by the government. Only after the war, when confronted with the atrocities committed by so many of my countrymen, did I once again entertain doubt about my parents. At that time, I still believed that Father was responsible for Leo's death after having witnessed the charade being played out about Änne's dismissal from our home years ago. Times were irrational all the way around. It became known that parents had denounced their children and vice versa for reasons unheard of before, because they supposedly undermined the stability of the Third Reich. Life and the individual had lost their raison d'être and had to be sacrificed and were, by a nation momentarily obsessed by the fanatical desire to please its leader.

CHAPTER 4

The Navy

The journey to Hamburg, where I was to report, went uneventfully except for many disturbing thoughts about the past. A fear of the unknown, plus my intense homesickness, made me almost regret the decision I had made so hastily. Certainly, no sense of patriotism had driven me to do what I had done, and so I had only my impatience to blame for my unhappiness. Things changed soon after my arrival when, with a group of other recruits, all two and three years older, I was sent to Denmark, a country under occupation. Our final destination turned out to be an equestrian academy on the outskirts of a city known to us as Sonderburg. The three-winged building where we stayed had a cobblestoned courtyard in the middle of beautiful countryside. Nearby stood a large hall with a high glass ceiling, which had been the equestrian school. We occupied one of the wings of the main building with the many other recruits who had arrived from different parts of the country for the purpose of being drilled for war. The central wing housed our officers and their staff, and the wing opposite ours was filled with *Kriegshelferinnen* (women in uniform, nurses, office personnel, and so on).

Our daily routine, like that of recruits all over the world, consisted of drilling, learning to clean our rifles, and learning all the other things recruits are required to know. We slept in bunks, twelve to a room, and after dinner there was always lots of dirty talk, card playing, swearing, and the lighting of farts, the humor of which eluded me completely. Because I was the youngest, very shy and quiet, they left me to myself. To show my appreciation, I began to smoke and drink beer.

After a few weeks, shortly before Christmas 1943, it was announced that a special gathering was to be held in the hall that demanded everybody's attention. The meeting concerned the upcoming Christmas party at which someone was needed to recite poetry, written for the occasion by one of our commanding officers. All possible candidates were to report that same evening.

It must have been survival instinct that turned me into a seasoned con artist in a matter of minutes. Not only did I come up with outrageous lies about my background, such as the one about Mother having taken me to acting and singing lessons since I was eight years of age, because she thought I had the talent to become a movie star, but I also proved to them there and then that I possessed a sort of seductive singing voice. My repertory consisted exclusively of popular songs sung by the then-famous movie queens, Zarah Leander and Marika Röck. The major and his staff were delighted with my renditions, especially with my declamatory reading of the major's poetry. I was hired, so to speak, on the spot. That Christmas Eve 1943 turned out to be my first success on a stage. I had chosen to have some well-known Christmas songs played ever so softly on a harmonica by a recruit from my group, while I recited at full force, not leaving a dry eye in that huge hall.

The repercussions from that evening turned out to be phenomenal. My life soon changed from being a recruit to being an entertainer. One of the wings of the academy had a small auditorium, and I was asked to produce an "Evening of Entertainment," using all available resources. I first made it known to the whole company that I was auditioning anyone who had, in the past, done anything remotely associated with the theatrical profession. To my surprise, there were enough musicians, amateurs but also some professionals, to put together a small musical ensemble, with one of the players acting as conductor. Not knowing anything about music, I nonetheless acted as director for the show I would soon attempt to bring to life. There were a number of guys who had worked as stagehands, some who confessed to being real acting students, and some who could sing and read a score. A few would-be designers filled out our group, and we all set out to put an "Evening of Entertainment" together. It goes without saying that everyone involved with the production also had to dance, sing, and participate in the sketches we were to devise. Besides acting as director, I also choreographed the dances and took part in several of the sketches. Always having been an avid moviegoer, I was able to retain melodies and words. I could recreate for myself the aura of certain dances from movies without having actually the ability to do the steps. But there I was, putting for the first time all my natural instincts into action without ever falling short of resources, and on top of it gaining the respect of the ones who knew much more than I. From now on, all of us involved in this project were excused after lunch from all duties except for the realization of our show. During morning drills, we were treated with respect by officers and recruits alike and talked about as "Artists."

Soon after we had arrived in Denmark, we had been told that the sailor's uniform would be ours to wear only after the completion of the training period. Meanwhile, we wore the same gray woolen uniforms as the rest of the army. To give our all-male revue an aspect of respectability, my suggestion to use exclusively the blue-and-white version of the navy's uniform was met with enthusiastic approval, after having gone through the appropriate channels, of course. After much trial and error, the final program turned out to be a fair mix of the serious and the absurd. An acceptable rendition of a Haydn string quartet and a pianist's rendering of a few pieces by Schumann made up the highbrow portion of the evening. Then, the full complement of musicians played Strauss waltzes, marches, and a few well-known operetta tunes, thus providing lighter fare. However, the rendering of some bawdy sketches, interspersed with my personal interpretations of some of the Leander and Röck songs, and the final dance number, ended the evening with the expected comic relief. The sketches, to which all participants had contributed, ranged from the ridiculous to the downright bawdy and hysterical and were, of course, the greatest hits. The evening became a huge success and had several more performances, one of them in a military hospital.

At the end of our drilling period in Denmark, we were sent to a new location in Germany for further instructions. Before being transported, we were entitled to a two-week leave to our respective homes. After we had reached German soil again, I boarded a train that took me to the Rheinland and Oberhausen. Eventually, passing through most of the north of the country, the train became overcrowded with travelers standing side by side in the aisles. All those people had come from the large cities in the industrialized part of the west to visit friends and family members with connections to farms, where they hoped to exchange anything disposable for things edible. On their way back home, it was possible to discern a sense of fear and chaos. Their faces revealed nothing of what they were thinking, and hardly a word was spoken. Some had chairs and other small furniture, stuffed into overhead compartments, things they had been unable to convert into foodstuffs. When changing trains and waiting for hours, I could hear and discern the intimate couplings in corners on the floor in the darkened station halls. People had lost all form of modesty because death had become a con-stant possibility. So much had been destroyed already. It was evi-dent that German morality was at a low point. All of this seemed to have happened during those last six or eight weeks while I had been in Denmark, out of touch with the rest of the world.

Mother, Father, and sister Änne were at home when I arrived. Father had recently returned home, after he had turned fifty years of age. Else and her baby had been evacuated, with many others, to relative safety in the south of Germany. As the Ruhr area was the most heavily industrialized part in the west of the country and under almost constant threat of bombardment, we decided, after I had spent a few days at home, that I should accompany Mother on the train to the village of Attenhofen near Ulm, where she could remain with her daughter and grandchild until the end of the war. That decision seemed to make it obvious that the idea of a lost war had taken hold in the minds of my family. We also knew of many others who had fled the big cities to await the end of the war in the less-populated places of our country. Much of Germany was in shambles by now, and hope for the German army's victory was vis-ibly eroding among the population. With most of the men gone to fight, only very young boys and older men stayed in towns and cit-ies as the last defenders of the Third Reich.

My family always had a dog and a cat. The dog belonged to Father, while I claimed the cat to be mine. Now I made it a point to take my cat on the trip south to save her from becoming food for the protein-starved population. My kit bag, fastened on top by a heavy cord, had been filled with my clothes, washed and freshly ironed. My cat had to be carried in a zippered handbag. With Mother carry-ing two small suitcases, we made it, via streetcar, to the train station and from there to the nearest city to board the connecting train to the south. Before boarding, it had become necessary to transfer my cat into my kit bag, on top of my clothes, because the zipper of the handbag had given away after repeated attempts by the frightened animal to escape her confinement.

The train had quickly filled to bursting, but we succeeded in occupying a corner at the end of one of the coaches, thus escaping being trapped in the overcrowded compartments. Sitting on our suitcases, I kept my kit bag between my knees, with one hand on top of the frightened cat. It was still early morning after the train had left the station, and soon people fell into a half sleep. After approximately one hour, our hopes of getting to our various destinations were smashed when, at various intervals, the train halted and orders were shouted to leave and seek shelter outside from approaching enemy planes. Most people literally threw themselves through windows and doors for fear of bombs or being hit by bullets. Mother and I, with a number of other passengers, stayed where we were. We reasoned that all the running around outside, looking for a place to hide, presented a far greater danger. After much delay and some fearful moments while we crouched at the sound of machine-gun fire, the train proceeded. Finally, we reached the major cities to the south, and, late at night, our own destination, the city of Ulm. We never learned about any possible casualties during our trip, and my very traumatized cat had survived.

From Ulm, a local train took us further into the countryside, but still several kilometers from the village of Attenhofen. In absolute pitch dark, carrying all our belongings, we attempted to find our way to my sister's temporary home, until a small streak of light revealed the presence of a house. Mother's timid knock on the door was rewarded with a welcoming voice from a farmer's wife who knew my sister. She insisted that we eat some supper and quickly produced homemade bread, real butter, ham, and other delicious cold cuts, all the things we had been deprived of for so long. Her determination to wash my soiled clothes, and my cat, had met with Mother's protest, but to no avail.

Our trip turned out to have a more than happy ending. Mother was able to spend the night sleeping on a sofa, with me curled up in blankets on the floor, while my cat enjoyed a bowl of real milk. During the early morning hours, we met the woman's husband, a farmer, who took us in his horse-drawn wagon the distance to our final destination. I am still profoundly embarrassed to admit to having forgotten our hosts' names. However, the encounter took place over sixty years ago, and, though even their faces have evaporated, the memory of it is still there.

Attenhofen was a charming, small farming community, with the unmistakable smell of cows and horses. Everyone seemed to know everyone, and my sister had become part of the community. After a few days at her home, when Mother had settled in and I had made sure that my cat had found a welcoming home, it was time for me to get back to my assigned post in Hamburg. From there, I was sent to an island in the North Sea.

CHAPTER 5
The Journey East

On the island of Rügen, on board a huge warship, we learned how to tie a sailor's knot, how to aim a cannon at an enemy's ship, and how not to become seasick. Being forced to spend twenty-four hours in the darkened, close space of a slowly undulating ship, we experienced what seemed endless hours of moaning and retching. Four weeks later, we had graduated, and a number of us were dispatched to Hamburg for a two-day rest before being sent further to an undisclosed destination.

At this time Hamburg, with its famous red-light district, and the *Reeperbahn*, with its sleazy stretch of bars and nightclubs, were magnets for sailors and soldiers on leave. In the red-light district, which was surrounded by a wall, the women exposed their wares behind shopwindows, on windowsills, and in doorways. The boys, starved for some sex and determined to visit one of the whorehouses, dragged me with them. My repulsion at the whole situation—the barely lit room, the unmade bed, and the large box of condoms on the night table, with the discarded ones visible in a wastepaper basket below—prompted me to tell my assigned fräulein a lie about an aunt who had passed away that same morning. In a conspiratorial way, she inquired if I was gay (*schwul*). The realization of that fact had not sunk in with me yet, and I answered in the negative, therefore also avoiding the danger associated with being found out.

When our two-day leave had come to an end, we reported to the train station at the appointed hour, where we and a large number of other sailors were ordered to board a special train that was to take us to that undisclosed place.

Traveling through unknown territory, gradually covered by a blanket of snow, we became aware that we were moving east. There were short, furtive stops at small stations with names nobody knew how to pronounce. Those stops, mostly at night, were accompanied by an eerie silence and no exchange of passengers. There was only the full moon and icy stillness and eventually the howling of wolves in the distance, but no visible lights to reveal any human presence. The landscape seemed frozen in time. Fresh snowfall painted the earth, and eventually the now sparse houses turned into small villages and cities. After having traveled for two days and two nights, we arrived at the station in Tallinn, then known as Reval, the capital of Estonia.

After we had been accommodated in a building at the center of the old town and assigned to our respective quarters, we were informed that our identity as sailors was to be kept a secret. We shed our uniforms and were given the gray ones accorded to all the other forces stationed on land. Until further notice, we were free to do as we pleased. Provided with food and a place to sleep, we were obliged only to sign in every twelve hours.

I soon set out to explore the charming old city. On my first excursion, I passed a tall building, which turned out to be Tallinn's opera house, and what I believed was the symphony hall. The opera house occupied the ground floor, while the symphony hall made its home above the opera house. On impulse, I purchased a ticket for that same evening. The program consisted of the opera *Pagliacci*, followed by a ballet titled *Autumn*, which I remember only as a sordid affair of falling leaves turning into willowing ballerinas. One of the women got repeatedly tossed into the air by a male leaf, which reminded me of a circus act I had once seen, except that the tossing had taken place on a tightrope, which had added considerably to the danger involved in catching the woman.

During the days that followed, I relished the discovery of this wonderful old city. Everything seemed very peaceful here, and in time I visited churches and museums and went to cinemas. Eventually, I became a guest at people's homes. One afternoon, in a large movie house, the screen burst into flames and panic ensued. People screamed and rushed towards the exit doors to be greeted outside with the sound of exploding bombs. The city was obviously under attack from Soviet planes. As we would learn later, firebombs had hit the roof of the theater. The façade of the building had thick columns, around which people draped themselves in rows of three and four. It was automatically assumed that the columns would stay in place should the building collapse. I had taken my place on one of the outer rows when I saw a plane diving dangerously low toward us from behind. The bomb missed its major target, but my upper right arm felt as if it had been hit by a stone. At the time, I gave it no further attention because, as soon as I could, I returned to headquarters, from which all of us were assigned to every part of the city to assist people in need of help. I helped move the wounded population into ambulances and carry furniture from burning buildings to safety, until my arm felt swollen and heavy. Back at headquarters, a doctor cut open the sleeve of my uniform. A piece of metal from a bomb had entered my upper arm. By now the wound had become infected, and I was sent by car to the nearest field hospital, approximately fifty kilometers from the smoldering city. Tallinn had been hit hard, and I left a cold and wounded town.

On arrival at the field hospital, I saw rows and rows of wounded soldiers, lying on stretchers and covered with blankets, in the snowy cold air. About six or seven houses, two and three stories high, stood in this beautiful pine tree–covered area overlooking the Gulf of Finland. Before the war, those houses had been vacation homes. Now they were turned into temporary hospitals for the wounded from the Russian front.

I soon found myself wheeled into a smoke-filled room with what looked like an improvised operating table, covered with a sheet that must have been in use for quite a number of other patients before me. Without much ado, I was placed on the table by two of the nurses. With only my jacket and undershirt removed and a mask placed over nose and mouth, I heard the words "count till ten." Just as I began to count, I felt the knife entering my arm. I woke in a large room with a glowing stove and a dozen or so other occupants. With a draining-tube protruding from my arm, daily rations of cigarettes, good food, excellent company, and the help of a wonderful German-speaking Russian nurse, I recovered in four weeks' time, after which I was sent back to Tallinn.

The mood had changed in the city. Gone was that sense of peace and calm that had made Tallinn so pleasurable. It was early summer by now, and families still ventured out to the banks of the river, where adults and children bathed in a picture of perfect harmony. But a kind of hush contributed to a sense of fear and uncertainty, in spite of the seeming peace surrounding us.

We had been put to work assembling parts that had been sent from Germany into small boats, just big enough for a crew of three. Those boats were to serve as minesweepers. On them we made the journey up the narrow river, more than halfway toward Europe's fourth-largest lake, the Peipus, which separated Estonia from the Soviet Union. A large green mansion, only about two hundred feet from the river, had been converted into our headquarters. Inside, the two stories of the house had been filled with bunk beds, covered with straw mattresses, inhabited by thousands of unruly mice.

Totally unafraid of our presence, they literally covered us whenever we tried to lie down. I moved out of the house and slept under the stars, as it was summer by now.

At night, our boats departed to the lake where, upon arrival, two of the boats would be connected by a cable before skimming part of the lake in total darkness, guided only by a compass. As dawn would break, we always found ourselves engulfed by a dense fog through which we had to find the entrance to the river and our way back to headquarters.

During the day, we mostly slept, when not on assignment to stand guard nearby over countless camouflaged boxes of ammunition. When our food supply dwindled, we were forced to consume part of our emergency field rations. The trucks in charge of making the trip from Tallinn once and sometimes twice weekly with food supplies had temporarily stopped making that trip. To reach us, they had to drive over mostly open terrain where they had lately been attacked several times by sniper planes. Meanwhile, we had begun the habit of searching for neighboring farms, removed from our base, where we would exchange blankets, sewing needles, and buttons for bread, butter, or a piece of ham. Perhaps four weeks after our arrival, word must have reached the Soviets about our whereabouts. Planes coming from the east flew over us regularly and must have been the same ones that had attacked the vehicles supplying our provisions. But with the house and the whole area covered by huge trees and our boats totally invisible from above, we did not suspect that we had been detected from the air but believed we had been informed on by one of the farmers. Being thus discovered had terrible consequences for us.

It had been my night to be shipped out, and for no reason other than a minor altercation with the corporal on our boat, I was assigned to stay guard at the base that night. Such an arrangement would leave me behind three nights instead of the usual two, when another crew was responsible for skimming the lake. The night was warm, and after only a short time of darkness past midnight, what seemed like a million frogs burst into song. As far as I could see, the ground was covered with them, causing me to stay in one spot until increasing light in the sky contributed to the gradual disappearance of frogs and song.

With the mouse activity getting worse inside the house, many others had decided to move outdoors. When I returned from guard duty that early morning, I remember us spending time talking and playing cards. When the hour arrived for the boats to be appearing back at our base, we grew increasingly worried, waiting. About one hour after the usual arrival time, two boats, severely damaged and with a number of wounded crew members on board, made it to our primitive landing dock. All other boats that had been out that night were lost, and presumably sunk, and the men on board with them. The two boats that escaped had stayed in the fog until the attacking planes had departed. Almost a third of our crew had vanished in the attack, and the loss of boats made our presence at the base obsolete. We were commanded to sit it out, as any rescue operation was impossible at the moment. The difficulty of our situation increased as the days passed without any news from the city. With emergency rations practically gone by now, some of us resorted to improvising soups made from water, grass, and weeds.

One early afternoon, the rumble of very low-flying planes from the east told us that something dangerous was approaching in our direction. Soon after our arrival many weeks ago, we had dug trenches about five hundred yards from the mansion. A number of us started to run toward the trenches just as the first bombs began to hit the compound and set the house aflame. Far enough removed from the central compound, the trenches ultimately provided safety for the ones who had reached them. But most were not that lucky, especially the ones caught asleep inside the house. While in the trench, I pressed myself against the ground, feeling the earth trembling. Counting the seconds and the bombs, falling in rapid succession, I remember feeling nothing at all, no fear, just hoping that the impact would be quick and painless. It all lasted no more than perhaps ten horrifying minutes. I survived with everyone who had made it to the trenches. When we finally dared to emerge, we saw only total destruction. There were fires and bodies everywhere. The sight of so many of our dead comrades, as well as survivors, unimaginably crippled in most cases, and the fact that our unit was devoid of real medical personnel, magnified the helplessness of our situation. We only cried while holding the dying in our arms so they would not have to die alone. Some took it upon themselves to tend to the wounded, providing only minor relief for lack of medication to ease their pain. At one point, while I was comforting a comrade behind a crumbling stone wall, a small fighter plane, with only the pilot and a machine-gun-wielding soldier clearly visible, passed over us from behind. The soldier saluted with his outstretched arm (the Nazi salute), while the pilot ascended into the sky, leaving us open-mouthed.

All communication through wire phones with Tallinn had been destroyed, and it took several days for some trucks to come to our rescue and drive us, those who were still alive, under almost constant machine-gun fire from diving planes, back to the city. We actually had to spend a lot of time jumping on and off the vehicles while shielding ourselves under bushes and in ditches.

On arrival, we learned that our unit had been moved somewhere between eight or ten kilometers east of the city into a number of barracks adjacent to the river. A few days later, it became obvious that the straw mattresses in our bunk beds were severely infected with crab lice (*Phthirus pubis*). Those vicious little creatures had invaded not just our pubic hair, but had taken hold under our arms and in our eyebrows. On a sunny day, we were all lined up to be completely shaved from head to toe, and to be soaked with a strong-smelling tincture that burned the skin and killed the parasites and their eggs. A huge bonfire took care of the mattresses, after which new bedding had to be improvised.

The Red Army was advancing westward with alarming speed, until it became necessary to install ourselves in trenches which we dug on the other side of the river. Only a few weeks later, the Soviets would occupy our barracks. They lost no time erecting a loudspeaker system on which they proceeded to transmit German popular music. Every once in a while, the music would be replaced by an announcement to inform us about the availability of caviar and champagne, along with the most beautiful Russian girls, just a hundred kilometers east in Leningrad. After several days of this charade, the news centered on the latest Soviet invention, an artillery piece named after Stalin, namely the "Stalin Orgel." That weapon turned out to be very destructive; once its shells reached our side, they shredded everything in sight. We had been approximately 150 sailors, and, as far as I could make out, only two of us escaped the massacre. The attack lasted about fifteen minutes, accompanied by the deafening sound produced by the continuous impact of those deadly weapons that would leave the area strewn with dead bodies.

After total darkness had set in, emerging from one of the trenches, I ran in the direction I thought would take me to the city. Eventually, I caught up with the sailor who was apparently the only other one who had escaped in the dark. At a certain point, we disagreed about which direction to take, and, as a result, we separated, never to see each other again. I do not remember what day or month it was, and do not think I knew then. The days had gotten shorter again, and some snow had fallen intermittently during the previous few days.

I ran over plowed fields covered partially with snow, in the process twisting my ankles this way and that, which considerably slowed my attempt at escape from the area. Whenever I heard the sound of cannons firing in the distance, I changed directions, which probably caused me to run in circles at times. When I spotted a cluster of isolated buildings, I believed I was in the outskirts of the city. No lights came from any of the houses, as the city must have been darkened so as not to be detected from the air.

After hours of running and walking, I had gotten very tired. Commanding all my courage, I knocked on the door of a large and isolated building on a deserted street corner. I was hoping for directions and perhaps some bread. The older woman who opened the door gestured for me to wait and disappeared. Shortly after, I was greeted by a tall woman with beautiful white hair gathered into a bun at the base of her neck. She was perhaps in her sixties, dressed in black, with a beautiful pale face dominated by large eyes whose color I was unable to discern in the darkish glow of light coming from behind her. In very educated High German, she invited me in. Contemplating my appearance, and before I was able to express my gratitude, she told me that I was welcome to stay overnight. She instructed the woman who had opened the door, a servant, to take me upstairs. The lady of the house invited me to take a bath while my clothes and shoes would be cleaned. Dinner was to be served at the late hour of 9:00 P.M.

The huge interior of the house was filled with oversized dark furniture. A sweeping carved wooden staircase led to the second floor and to my assigned room. Inside, a framed mirror twice my size, an ornate bed, some chairs, a writing table, and an armoire filled the somewhat dimly lit interior. A sliding door led to a bathroom with the largest freestanding tub I had ever seen.

I had experienced the friendliness Estonians displayed towards us Germans, and through my contact with the people of Tallinn, it was obvious that Russians were not welcomed there. Still, we were the occupying force and, therefore, the enemy. So why was I treated like that? I never had had the luxury of a real bathtub, or any bathtub, period. At home, we had taken our baths in a zinc barrel, barely large enough to sit in with knees pulled up to our chest. Now, lying completely covered under soothing hot water, I felt like a king in a fairy tale. A male servant had discreetly removed my clothes and shoes. Shortly after I had emerged from my bath, I found my uniform brushed clean, and my underwear and soiled pieces of cloth, our substitute for socks, washed and still warm from having been freshly ironed. I dressed, and shortly after was reminded that I was expected downstairs for dinner. Descending the stairs, I was shocked to see the hostess in evening dress and two old gentlemen in their tuxedos. We briefly shook hands, but I was never enlightened as to who they were.

After having taken our places at a big wooden table, I discovered to my horror a number of knives and forks placed beside a beautiful array of china. The male servant entered and, in absolute silence, placed a slice of toasted bread on each plate. The hostess, lifting a fork and a knife, and in so doing indicating to me which one to use, proceeded to cut the bread. And so with fork and knife we ate the bread as if it had been a piece of meat. With our eyes downcast and no word spoken, it all felt like some sort of ritual, and it dawned on me that this family, or what was left of it, tenaciously and with absolute faith, stuck to its ancestral customs.

The servant, having collected our plates and used silverware, replaced them with new ones. Now entering with a bowl of steaming hot potatoes, he ceremoniously deposited one of them on each plate. With only a slight sprinkling of salt, we consumed the potato as slowly as possible. Occasionally, we would lift our gaze and nod our heads in approval of what nature had provided. There was total silence, never any encouragement to talk, just to worship. After yet another change of plates, a small bowl of dried apple slices had made the rounds and a cup of steaming hot tea signaled the end of the meal. When the lady of the house rose from her seat, it all came to an end. After a respectful bow to each other, we all departed to our rooms. On the bed, a nightgown had been laid out for me, and, in very little time, I fell into a deep and satisfying sleep.

After a knock on the door, the male servant made it clear to me that I was expected downstairs with all my belongings. I dressed in a hurry and collected my few possessions.

Descending the stairs, I found the clock in the hall showing the time at 5:00 A.M. The maidservant walked me wordlessly to the entrance door, indicating that I was to depart. It was obvious that this abrupt decision to have me leave so unceremoniously had its reason after such heartfelt welcome the day before. Fear must have played a part and the knowledge, perhaps through the news on the radio, about the Soviet Army's rapid approach toward the west. To be found playing host to a German soldier would obviously have endangered their lives.

I had forgotten to ask for directions and walked very fast toward the countryside, still farther away from the city. In the early afternoon, I encountered a large farmhouse with other retreating German soldiers who had escaped the Soviets from various other fronts. Perhaps twenty or twenty-five of them, they seemed to have no visible leadership and didn't know what to do next. Finally, I left the building undetected through a back door and continued walking until I had made contact with another unit on their way to the port of Paldiski, about fifty or sixty kilometers from Tallinn. I became aware that I had traveled much farther than I had assumed, for I learned that only about thirty kilometers ahead of us lay the port city. More and more soldiers and officers joined us as we were heading toward the Gulf of Finland, followed by civilians in cars and on bicycles. Everybody seemed to be heading for the port in the hope of an escape from the Red Army. All of us, hundreds by now, soldiers and sailors alike, were soon formed into a mixed unit commanded by some of the officers.

On arrival at the port, we witnessed the pandemonium that had broken out. Two large ships lay at the pier, and we were ordered to help transport the many wounded, arriving in a never-ending column in Red Cross vehicles, to one of the ships that had been designated exclusively for the wounded, the doctors, and the nurses. The ship, identified as *Lazarettschiff* (military hospital ship), had great respect from the civilian population, which seemed to increase by the minute. It was the second ship that stirred people's emotions because it had been made available to the Estonian population who wished to go to Germany to become part of the work force, in addition to the retreating German Army. People left their cars and bicycles and tried to sell their jewelry and other worthwhile possessions before boarding the ship. After we had loaded the last wounded soldiers on board, the *Lazarettschiff* left, only two hours ahead of us.

It was still daylight when we lifted anchor. We sailors stayed together, reporting to each other our adventures. I learned that there had been much maritime activity along the coast, and we all deplored our departure from the area. One sailor carried his guitar with him, and we sang together until late at night, to the merriment of the many civilians surrounding us under a starry sky and on a by now high sea. Nobody knew about our exact destination, except for the fact that we were headed for German soil. We had been advised to provide our own food for the journey, as there would be no distribution of food items on board. And, of course, there were constant long lines to reach any sanitary facility. It became necessary simply to wait in line until the urge would make itself felt. After several days, meeting people, playing cards, singing, joking, and doing all the things one does in those situations had lost their ability to entertain, and clouds had begun to form. That sense of relief, which had been so palpable during those last days, was disappearing. A fear of the unknown had set in, and maybe also our by now self-imposed rationing of food items and cigarettes contributed to a general low morale among all passengers. Information from above was not forthcoming, and the realization that the trip might take considerably longer than had been estimated beforehand did nothing to improve the situation. Although we still sang songs, especially in the evenings, they had become sad songs, devoid of optimism and joy.

Several days later, rumors began to circulate that after one more night we were to drop anchor in Germany. Unable to search for any clues, we waited and hoped for another two days. I have conflicting recollections about the city where we finally disembarked. I tend to think it was Königsberg, now Kaliningrad. However, it could have been the nearby city of Gdansk, known to us as Danzig until 1945. Sometime later we were informed about the tragic disappearance of the *Lazarettschiff*, not long after its departure from the port of Paldiski. The ship had succumbed to an enemy torpedo attack and consequently had sunk. I am also in the dark as to what happened to the Estonian population and all the returning ground troops after we had left the ship. Without delay, we sailors were taken to a school building that was to serve as our temporary quarters until it would be decided what to do with us next. It was the end of 1944, and I remember spending New Year's Eve on a U-boat at a party to which I had been invited with one of our commanding officers with whom I had become friendly. It turned out to be a wild drinking party to which I totally succumbed and where I remember having danced with most of the ship's crew. The following morning my officer friend had dragged me back to our temporary housing, where I was left on a pile of straw.

The German navy must have lost its fleet by now, and consequently we were assigned to replace the much-needed ground troops on the eastern front. The weather had turned bitterly cold. We were totally in the dark as to which part of the front we had been transported to; we waited for our next assignment. No special instructions had been given, other than to stay on guard on an icy terrain, where in the distance it was possible to see the flashes of cannons firing in the night. Every two hours, my vigil was taken over by a comrade who had been asleep in a hole dug in the ground and filled with straw. I had to shake him awake, and the moment he emerged, it was my turn to fall into the hole. I was already asleep before hitting the ground, in spite of the many vermin inhabiting the pile of straw. Every two hours, that procedure repeated itself throughout the night. The reason for the presence of the two of us at this particular place was never revealed to us. We had been assigned to stand guard where there was nothing to be guarded, until we were called to join yet another group and sent to a place farther east.

On the edge of a dense pine forest, we dug trenches again. The earth being frozen solid made that chore extremely difficult, and the minimum depths had to reach four feet. Fighting not just the hard soil, our small pick-axes struggled with the powerful roots from the tall trees surrounding us. Under constant heavy snow, we finally spent a whole week in those trenches, expecting an encounter with the advancing Red Army. As there was no supply of food besides our meager field rations, some very courageous souls ventured overnight to a nearby abandoned farm. Its owners had fled, and the harrowing, constant sounds of unmilked cows and other animals without feed had gotten our attention. Soon we found ourselves in the possession of a slaughtered pig. All of the other animals gradually perished, and after a few more days we found ourselves surrounded by a ghostly silence. During daylight, we succeeded in lighting a small fire in one of the trenches with some of the brush from the forest, and everyone cut himself a piece of meat from the slowly smoldering flesh of the pig. Hunger, impatience, and that impossible little fire prevented the meat from becoming sufficiently roasted, and so it was consumed practically raw and cold. Tired and freezing from standing in the snow-filled trenches, we kept running in place to keep our circulation going. Suddenly, out of nowhere, a group of High German officers clad in heavy fur-collared military coats approached us from behind. One of them, introduced to us as General Schwartz, was paying us a visit to congratulate our unit for its bravery. After the usual pep talk, we were invited to a retreat a few kilometers back in the woods, where we could enjoy a good night's sleep.

The officers led us through the thickness of the dense forest and, wonder of wonders, after only an hour we arrived at an underground bunker, clearly a refuge for the officers. The bunker felt terribly overheated after we had been exposed to temperatures far below zero degrees for such a long time. The heat emanated from a wood-burning stove in a corner, and, after having been assigned a cot of my own, I removed only my boots before falling into a deep and dreamless sleep.

Just a few minutes seemed to have passed when I was awakened. Orders were given to be at the ready, as a new defense strategy had been developed for our unit. Unable to fit my now swollen feet back into the boots, I was given a very large pair made of felt. After having received some new field rations, we were led to yet another place to confront the Red Army.

The place resembled a cutoff mountaintop, which we climbed in order to take our positions on its rim. There was only open field in front of us, and in the distance it was possible to make out the edge of a forest through which the enemy was supposedly advancing toward us. Below, on our left, a large river as wide as the Rhein looked totally frozen. Very dense snow blew in our direction, which made for zero visibility, and soon the order was given to open fire. Not being able to see anything ahead, most of us just lay there, waiting, while a few fanatics shot their guns into the empty space. Nothing happened, and after a while, tired and cold, I must have drifted into a temporary sleep. Not having noticed that my unit had gotten the order to descend, or perhaps retreat, I found myself alone when I opened my eyes again. When I lifted my head and turned around, I witnessed my entire unit being led away by the Soviets at the foot of the mountain. Undetected, I lay down flat until I made sure that everyone had disappeared. I slid down the mountain, ran to the nearby river, and, after jumping onto the ice, landed knee-deep in water. Obviously, the ice on the edge of the river had not been frozen deep enough to hold my weight, but I made it to the top. When I was halfway across the river, my escape was discovered, and bullets chased me into the forest on the other side. Pure instinct made me run in a direction I hoped would not lead me into the arms of another group of enemies.

Again, it was a very long walk, a whole day until late that night, through fields and forests. In the end, I reached some houses in a small village. Hearing noises and detecting a ray of light from one of the windows, I was able to spot a room full of older German soldiers. I knocked on the door and was welcomed into the smoke-filled room like a lost son. They lavished bread, canned sardines, beer, and cigarettes on me, and I answered all their questions. These men were Germany's last hope to stall disaster. None of them had any idea how far away the front was and how bad the situation was out there. I told them all I knew and what happened to me and all my comrades back in Estonia. Seeing that I was tired and spent, they finally insisted that I rest. Trying to shed those big felt boots, I realized it was impossible. With scissors and knives, the men cut the boots open, which revealed my blackened, frostbitten, and very swollen feet and lower legs.

Now everyone got into the action, constructing a device that resembled a pair of crutches built from boards that would at least get me to the nearest field hospital, to which some of the men took me the following morning.

At the hospital, I stayed only long enough to have my feet and lower legs covered with powder. Wrapped in bandages and provided with a pair of real crutches and a sign around my neck that read simply "wounded," I was deposited on a corner where the next passing military truck would pick me up to drive me to a station just a few kilometers away. On arrival at the station, I was surprised to find hundreds of other wounded soldiers waiting for the train that was to take us all to a real hospital. Red Cross workers handed out sandwiches and coffee but had no information as to when or where the train would take us. For many hours, some of us shared individual stories, laced with the hopes of a speedy recovery, while others, too tired or depressed because of the loss of a leg or an arm or perhaps both, just lay wordless on their stretchers, inhaling the smoke from cigarettes held for them by nurses and soldiers.

CHAPTER 6

The Journey West

Finally, a heavily puffing locomotive, hauling approximately ten or twelve passenger cars, came into view alongside the platform. After all the wounded had been loaded on board, the train departed at sundown, at a snail's pace and, as we would soon discover, without medical personnel or medication for the ones who depended on it. The conductor of the train had made it known that his instructions had been to head west, away from the front. As he was the only employee on the train, it was necessary for him to stop often, in order to feed the locomotive. It also became the order of the day to retreat whenever the sound of cannons made it apparent that we were heading in the wrong direction. In that case, the train had to move backwards again, always at a slow pace, until the conductor had found the junction that would take us in the right direction. After two days and nights when we were squeezed together in the overcrowded compartments without food and half asleep, the train screeched alongside an open platform. To our relief, the place was swarming with Red Cross personnel ready to ladle some warm soup into any container we carried with us. A large number had to be fed, and whoever could walk would take on that task. However, in the process it was discovered that some of the severely wounded had died. Consequently, we emptied several compartments to accommodate the dead for the rest of the journey.

On the platform of this small town, whose name I do not remember, I speculated on the reality that Germany was losing the war, wondering how it all would end. Before I left home, Father had promised me that I could study acting at the renowned *Folkwangschule* when the war was over. But when would that be? In little more than a month, I would be turning nineteen, and I still hadn't done very much with myself. I wished so much for the war to be over.

The train stopped at many other small stations, sometimes for many hours and always greeted by Red Cross personnel. There would be soup, sometimes sandwiches, but sometimes only coffee would be left. By now, on only our fourth day, one whole car had been emptied to accommodate the dead. It would take another two days before, late one evening, the train rolled into the station of a major city. Word of our imminent arrival had gotten around fast, and we were jubilant. Before we had come to a complete standstill, a loudspeaker system informed us not to leave the train. We would have to continue until we reached the next city, as all the hospitals were overfilled. Doctors and nurses on the platform tried in vain to calm a number of wounded who had left the train, defying the order to stay inside. There ensued arguments with the military police. Taking advantage of the general confusion, I reasoned that if I managed to hobble fast enough into the nearest men's room, I had a chance to make it eventually to a local hospital. After about half an hour, I heard the unmistakable sound of the departing train. Presuming that doctors and nurses were still on the platform, I left the men's room and positioned myself in the middle of the road outside the station in front of several ambulances stationed there.

It took longer than I had expected for the medical personnel to leave the station because the dead had to be loaded into special vans. But now, the headlights of the first ambulance fell on me, crouching in the middle of the street holding up my crutches. My presence produced consternation, soon to give way to the inevitability of the fact that I was there. On the trip to the hospital, the nurses expressed relief that not more of us had escaped. The hospital was full to bursting, with every corridor filled with emergency cots, and two of the nurses had to share one bed to make room for me. The doctors turned out to be local folk, but the nurses had been recruited from everywhere and needed to stay at the city's various hospitals to be on call at any time. This shortage of space had also required that the hotels in the city be converted into temporary convalescent centers.

After eight days, we all were loaded into cattle cars to be shipped farther west, away from the advancing Red Army. This time we traveled lying on straw covered with blankets. I remember fighting a high fever combined with a splitting headache during most of that trip. We stopped only once or twice before we arrived in Hamburg. I ended up in a large hospital room with at least a dozen beds, occupied by soldiers of all ages. For the next five weeks, with my legs suspended in the air by pulleys, this room became my home. By now my feet had turned completely black, shriveled and wrinkled, and been declared frozen to a third degree.

During my last week at the hospital, I was informed that it had become necessary to amputate my toes the following day. Then, with a special pair of shoes, I should be able to walk like a normal person. An alarm went off in my head, and during the night, with only a pair of tweezers in my possession, I peeled away a large part of the dead, black flesh from one of my large toes. After probing carefully through a layer of very bad-smelling pus, I discovered something pink, only half the size of my toe as I knew it and without a toenail. I had exposed a new toe. Although the toe was deprived of any feeling when touched, I immediately alerted the night-nurse, who in turn informed the doctor on call, and at the earliest hour I found myself being wheeled into the operating room. Here my feet were stripped of all the dead tissue, revealing new, little, rosy toes. The smallest ones were actually missing, except for the bare bones. The medical men, pretending to be in utter disbelief, predicted, however, that all my toes would grow back to their original size in just a matter of time. As for now, equipped with a pair of crutches, I was released and sent to join my sister Else with child and Mother in Attenhofen, for a period of recovery.

The western part of Germany had already been occupied by American, British, and French troops while the Soviets were invading the country from the east. Only a narrow part of Germany was still accessible for travel, with people and their belongings atop the coal being transported by train. The only passenger car was reserved for soldiers traveling south. No sign of alarm was part of that trip, and in relative comfort I arrived in Ulm and ultimately in Attenhofen. I had avoided informing parents and sisters about my hospital confinement, and so my arrival on crutches was understandably greeted with dismay, but that feeling was dispelled after my account that nothing was missing from my body and that my feet were only in need of daily treatment with some special powder to keep the injured skin dry. I had to report every week to the nearest military post in Ulm, where a doctor would determine my future ability to serve the German army. On one of those visits, I spent several hours in a jail, while my sister Else hurried to my rescue, producing the necessary identification papers I had forgotten at home.

After four weeks, I was able to walk without crutches and after yet another week was declared fit enough to work as a clerk in a military office. I do not remember having ever been assigned any task at this office, as we would soon be constantly on the move, joined by a number of other units, retreating farther and farther south into

Tyrol. While passing through one of the small towns, we learned that Hitler was dead, but no further detail revealed the circumstances. The Allied troops were not far behind us, although we did not know it then, and on a beautiful spring day we were ordered to transport all our leftover munitions, supplies, and food items up into the alps. Mules, which had been confiscated from surrounding farms, were guided by us up the narrow steep passage into the snow-covered alps. The animals had been loaded with provisions, mostly flour and some canned goods, from the vehicles below. Halfway up that narrow lane, the landscape had become totally snowbound, which made it extremely difficult for animals and humans to proceed. At the final destination, a large barn, the snow reached above our knees. The air was thin up there, and after repeated trips there seemed to be nothing to do. We idled the days away, while a few fanatic officers insisted on giving orders. Part of the day was spent looking for anything to burn in a wood stove in the middle of the barn, and corned beef was all we consumed during those days. A little more than a week had passed when we were told that the war was over and that we could go home.

CHAPTER 7

The End of World War II

With the prospect of going home and the sun shining in a cloud-less sky, most of us couldn't contain the joy such news meant to us. The descent to the world below became a race as to who would hit the road to our respective homes first. After the long descent, at the street below and with my kit bag slung over my shoulder, I set out to find whatever would transport me to the vicinity of Ulm or Attenhofen. Not having ever experienced anything similar and with absolute naivete, I treated the news of the end of the war simply with joy, like any other good news. In total innocence, I disregarded the consequences of a war lost. A large number of strange-looking vehicles (Jeeps) passed me by, occupied by black, smiling soldiers who waved me on. And then, just as I walked around a curve in the road, several large military trucks and a group of what seemed to be American soldiers with rifles slung over their shoulders were waiting. Of course, all of us who had walked in that direction were stopped here. After they poked through our luggage, which in my case contained nothing more than some underwear and a few bars of soap, we were loaded onto trucks. Unfortunately, I also had been relieved of my watch that had been a present from Leo after I had won that regional ice-skating championship. We were taken to a large and open expanse of land that was to become our POW camp. For several weeks, we slept on grass and in the open, but during my two months in the camp the sun shone hot and merciless every day. At one point, we were supplied with tents, and fences were built around us. Once in a while, the Americans would use a fire hose to spray water into our compound and then, stark naked, we would wash ourselves and dance and sing.

A translator was assigned to explain to us that there was no food available to be distributed. The transport of supplies was too slow for the rapidly advancing army. To alleviate the situation, the Americans offered to accompany a few from our group, those familiar with our previous hideouts, to recover what perhaps had been left or lay forgotten in the mountains. They returned with several sacks of flour which, after having been delivered to a baker in a nearby village, were turned into bread that provided nearly five hundred POWs with at least a mouthful. Hunger was always with us, until a deal was made between the American administration and the farmers in the area to use us, supervised, as farmhands. For this service, we were rewarded at the end of each day with a thick slice of still warm, hearth-baked bread.

While we were in the camp, and with nobody ever visibly guarding us, word got around that some POWs had broken through the fence at one corner that bordered on clumps of bushes and trees. A small path had led them to a village at night, where they had begged and received some food. The path, thick with brush and difficult to maneuver, did not prevent me from trying my luck one night. All by myself, halfway through the thick brush, I got lost, turned around, and suddenly found myself confronted by two black soldiers leaning against their vehicle, grinning broadly. After I had formed the word "jail" in my mind, I was reminded that this was going to be a friendly encounter. "Fräulein, eh?" was all they could pronounce, and after I quickly reaffirmed that statement, they handed me two oranges, the likes of which I hadn't seen since the war began. They made it clear to me that I was to eat them right there and, after having smoked the cigarette offered, I understood that I was to keep my mouth shut. I thanked those two wonderful people and made my way back to the camp, hearing them laugh behind me.

After two months in the camp with the constant sun beating down on us, my hair had become almost white, hanging to my shoulders. The color of my skin resembled that of a mulatto. I hardly recognized myself in the mirror in one of the barracks erected for the process of our "denazification." Huge books lay in front of a number of uniformed specialists who seemed to have carefully studied my background, that of my parents, and who knows what else. This personal examination lasted perhaps an hour or so and was conducted in a perfectly respectful manner. After having received my Certificate of Discharge and a thorough medical exam, I, like everyone else, was given one whole loaf of bread (the kind that turns into a little ball when squeezed), along with a piece of butter. Shortly after we had consumed the bread and butter, the line leading to the latrine grew long very quickly.

Several military trucks were waiting to transport us to the cities closest to our homes in the south of Germany, and so, after reaching the city of Ulm, I was set free. On my way to the station, a car occupied by two American officers flagged me down. Asked where I was going, I responded to the one who spoke almost perfect German, that my family in the village of Attenhofen was in the dark about my whereabouts and that that was where I was heading. Needless to say, the invitation to jump into the back seat brought me to my sister's place in no time, and before I was given the chance to thank them, I was given several bars of chocolate.

Back at my sister's temporary home in Attenhofen, Mother, Else, and I eagerly awaited the day when we would be able to embark on the trip back to our own home in Oberhausen. Ultimately, we had to delay our return for several more weeks, as any travel by train right after the war was an impossibility. In the end, we traveled the approximately seven to eight hundred kilometers mostly on top of slow-moving transport trains filled with coal, along with many others returning to various cities in the west. Parting had not been easy, as the elderly couple who owned the house to which my sister had been assigned had become attached to Mother, Else, and especially Else's child. They were a very gentle older couple.

Our arrival in Oberhausen, which was now in West Germany, was greeted by handshakes, not hugs, and an immediate assessment of damage to our house. When I think back even now, what strikes me most about my German family is the absence of emotional demonstrations. We never did, nor was I taught to do, any hugging or kissing. At this writing, I remember that such manifestations were always strictly reserved for babies and dogs.

Some windows of the house had burst from the pressure of the bombs that had fallen in the vicinity. Änne had repaired them with pieces of cardboard. Actually, very little had been targeted in our area. Only one house, separated from us by maybe one hundred feet of lawn, had been hit by firebombs and partially burned.

With the war over, people's main occupation now became what is universally known as picking up the pieces. The lack of practically everything drove us to become cunningly inventive in finding and stretching any available food items. It became a common habit to travel for hours on overflowing trains and stand on platforms, rain or shine, like sardines in a can. Perhaps an old overcoat or whatever seemed dispensable could be exchanged for a few potatoes, some butter, a few eggs, or a piece of ham. The many small farms north of us were the victims of us beggars from the cities. Not far from home, actually a part of our community, was a large coal mine where, after darkness had set in, mysterious shadows appeared carrying buckets in the hopes that the departing trains would drop some of their cargo, which to everybody's great joy happened frequently. It was not enough to fill the containers once, but, after numerous visits to that site, my family didn't have to fear the coming of winter. Of course, winters were spent in the small kitchen, economizing on that prized black gold.

The usual chaos in times like these, before the bureaucratic machine had been made to function again, led to a great deal of corruption. I witnessed the illegal dealings in the distribution of coupons for gasoline. Though it was a highly rationed commodity, it presented no problem for Änne. She was in the process of establishing her own small business again, selling fruits and vegetables. Her acute ability to strike business deals made her the only really successful person in our family. Even fruits and vegetables were still items requiring ration coupons, and her dealings on the flourishing black market eventually made her a rich woman. Änne's individually polished apples, presented on a piece of black velvet, attracted only the highest-paying customers. Always dressed immaculately, she delivered the goods personally to her most important customers.

After Leo's death, Änne had gone through an emotionally turbulent time, after which she had married a German officer who was also the spiritual leader of a secret sect, to the dismay of the rest of our mainstream Christian family. I met him only fleetingly while on leave, before accompanying Mother on her way to Attenhofen. They had two daughters, Ursula and Gerda, before he died of cancer. Father and Else's husband Josef had returned from the war unscathed. Father had actually been sent home when he turned fifty years of age, to serve at the home front in the *Sicherheitshilfsdienst*, a sort of service for all kinds of local emergencies, which lasted until the war ended. He then had to go through all the legal channels before he was allowed to reopen his business. Josef, for his part, remained Father's right hand, just as Else would later on when Mother retired from her chores.

CHAPTER 8

At the Folkwang School

As for my part of the story, it did not take me very long, a couple of months at most, before I reminded Father of his promise to let me study acting at the Folkwang School. He must have hoped that my infatuation with the theater had ended with the end of the war. My reminder elicited a curt answer: "Why don't you just go and ask if they are interested in you?" I thought it a reasonable answer and prepared myself to take the train the very next morning to Essen-Werden, which had become the newly appointed seat of the school. It was by now early November and unseasonably cold. Most of the passenger trains still had no glass in their windows, and the signs of the war just past were everywhere in evidence. But the famous German *Pünktlichkeit* (being on time) had already been restored to its former glory. For me, that fateful trip turned out to be uneventful, cold, and almost three hours long. After changing trains twice, I arrived at about 9:30 A.M.

Asking directions to the school, I walked the short distance to the building that would change my life. The moment I stepped on its cobblestoned courtyard, I noted the gaping holes where windows should have been. Suspiciously, I walked towards the heavy central entrance door of the building, hoping that it would open. To my relief, it did. I could make out the faint sound of piano playing in the dark interior and to my right the open door over which the word *Büro* (office) was posted. I knocked on the door frame of a small room where an elderly lady sat behind a desk laden with papers. A sweet and welcoming voice asked me to enter, and when she inquired about the motive of my visit, I told her, "I want to be an actor." With a faint smile and infinite patience, she explained that the building had just only now been assigned to house the Folkwang School. With the war barely over, no decisions in regard to the teaching personnel had been made yet, and classes for all departments would not start before the beginning of the coming year. She did offer me, however, an application form for later consideration. After explaining to her that my father in all probability would not let me come again, and after begging for some official document that would at least indicate my future acceptance, she revealed to me that at 11:00 A.M. an audition was being held for the dance division, which I would be welcome to attend.

Not knowing anything about dance, or even its existence as an art, in spite of a number of classes I had attended four years earlier to improve my ice-skating skills, I accepted the offer with a sort of what-the-heck attitude. Once having been accepted into the school, I hoped it would always be possible to switch to another department. The audition took place in a different wing of the building on the second floor, with two columns in the middle of the studio and a coal-burning stove in a corner. After being ushered in, I met the two dance teachers and the pianist. There were other judges, heads of the music and art department, as I was to learn afterwards, and all were seated behind several large tables with pen and paper poised to determine admission to that prestigious school. The other applicants, about a dozen of them and all girls with ominous expressions, wore long skirts in darkish colors for the audition. All I could do was to remove my shoes and socks on the advice of one of the girls. We were asked to skip and walk to the different speed and rhythm of the music being played. Finally, we were asked to improvise individually. When my turn arrived, I was asked to fight an unseen wild animal. My performance over, Trude Pohl, who later would become my teacher, inquired if it had been a chicken I had had in mind.

My having been the only boy at the audition must have determined the judges' decision to accept me on a three-month probation period. As school was not to begin until after the New Year had started, I promised myself privately to improvise and improve on my fighting abilities. At home, announcement of my acceptance did not result in spontaneous jubilation, but, for me, the determination to succeed in an area I didn't know anything about would quickly take hold of me. I had danced on ice, which had taken the fear out of spinning and jumping and moving in general, but now I would learn to dance on a stage where I so badly longed to be. Still, the only dancing I had seen, which had definitely not been to my liking, had been on my first night as a sailor in Tallinn. But, after more thorough investigation about dance in Germany, I discovered the existence of a dancer by the name of Harald Kreutzberg, and, judging from his photographs, he resembled nothing that I had seen on the stage before. I secretly hoped that this was the kind of dance with which I was going to be made familiar.

At the beginning of 1946 when classes had finally begun, I learned that all the girls who had auditioned traveled, like me, in different directions after a day of classes. All of them had had previous dance experience, especially one of them, Gisela Asteroth, who had come from the Wigman School in Dresden. We became fast and close friends and later danced together professionally for several years. After only a short time, it had become obvious that I had surpassed all my teacher's expectations, especially in ballet technique. My ice-skating skills had at least given me an excellent jump-start on my future career. No word was ever mentioned again about my probation period, a fact I wisely had not disclosed to my family. My original wish to become an actor vanished soon after I had experienced the total physical involvement demanded by the training for a career in dance.

Trude Pohl became more than my dance teacher. She took it upon herself to educate me in matters of literature and music, especially about writers, poets, and composers whose works had been prohibited during the Nazi reign. Together we attended a performance of Hindemith's *Mathis der Maler* and many concerts with the works of composers not heard in German concert halls for many years. I discovered Thomas Mann, whose writings would occupy a special place among my newly acquired treasures. However, my major assignments would consist of reading through the works of the great Greek philosophers and poets. Frau Pohl, as we addressed her, made sure that we constantly worked on the dances she had assigned to us. During one week, we were given music to make a dance that would demonstrate the progress we had made technically, while the following week was spent on a dance for which we were given a specific theme that was to challenge our imaginations. Eventually, however, all those restrictions would be eliminated, and the dances we made became personal statements.

After classes, most of us would gather in the train station's restaurant. After each of us had contributed one of the then-assigned ration coupons, we would order a terrine of soup containing a few pieces of potatoes and some leafy green vegetables. The waitress, like all waiters and waitresses at the time, sold black-market cigarettes. One single cigarette had to make the rounds among the six or eight of us who had willfully missed another train in order to spend time together to discuss the day's work.

Solo concerts by modern dancers were still very much in vogue. Trude Pohl herself gave several concerts, which drew me into a world I had not imagined possible. She seemed flawless to me, in a perfectly dramatic personification of the Greek tragic persona Niobe, who had murdered her seven children. Surrounded by just black velvet curtains, moving her beautifully expressive arms and hands, sculptured by lighting, at once mysterious and awesome, she became the heroine she dared to portray. I became her ardent admirer and worked very hard to be worthy of her attention. She took me to a concert given by Harald Kreutzberg. Kreutzberg, by then already at an age when all great performing artists begin to be at war with themselves, had developed a visible paunch. Although his prowess as a performer was unmistakably intact, I was unable to ignore the fact that his body was not anymore that of an athlete, which a number of photographs in the program attested to. He possessed the most beautiful and expressive hands, which he used to great advantage in his dances, which were of a wondrous variety. He set himself apart from all other solo dancers in that he was able to distill emotion perfectly into original and beautiful characterizations that spoke volumes throughout the world.

Gret Palucca, another notable German solo dancer of an earlier period whom we saw in concert, demonstrated a completely different aspect of the modern dance of that time. Palucca's dances were musical visualizations. I remember them as perfectly structured affairs, the soloist always in the center with a small corps moving behind in counterpoint and other musical configurations. She was known to be a great jumper and did so in all the dances on the program I saw. There were no men in her company then. I remember the costumes worn by the women: long skirt, naked midriff, and tight-fitting sleeveless top. All the dancers wore the same pastel color, which changed with each of the dances. Palucca avoided emoting of any kind and thus was perhaps the most advanced of the moderns of the time.

Finally, another male student entered the dance division of the school. Also during this time, I met Kurt Jooss, who with his company had fled Nazi Germany and found a new home in Dartington, England. His company, Ballet Jooss, was now performing for the British troops in Germany, and he made it a point to visit the dance division of the school he had founded. Trude Pohl, who had been a member of his original company, introduced him to us. During the war years, Jooss had become a huge name in dance throughout the world. His works, *The Green Table* and *Big City*, choreographed in 1932, were then, and continue to be today, widely performed. I was horrified to discover that Trude had invited him to watch me perform a dance I had choreographed.

Father was now back in business, and I only saw him on weekends when he seemed too tired even to go to his soccer game. He would sleep instead. Being back in business didn't mean much to the normal folks, who still had to buy produce with their allotment of coupons, while my family didn't have to suffer those shortcomings anymore. Sometimes I would ask Mother for some carrots or potatoes to take to my teacher, but only on rare occasions did I succeed in getting them.

During my daily trips to and from Essen-Werden, I had become acquainted with a number of my fellow travelers. With some of them, I would engage in casual sex in the many burnt-out buildings, which for a long time served as ideal places for fast and unencumbered sexual encounters among homosexuals and heterosexuals alike. At one time, one of them had me disembark with him in one of the cities en route to my hometown. I knew the city vaguely because in the beginning of the war I had visited there frequently and remembered so many of its buildings surrounding the station.

There had been a small restaurant on a corner that had been leveled to the ground toward the end of the war. My companion led me through the rubble of the burnt-out area until we reached the point where I thought the restaurant had been. To my surprise, he pointed to an opening in the ground where, in the dark, it was possible to discern some light coming from beneath. I followed him down a ladder into what must have originally been a basement. When he opened a door, I found myself confronted with a large group of men engulfed in smoke, standing around a makeshift bar, drinking and conversing by candlelight. I found out that the restaurant I remembered had been a gay meeting place until war's end, to be given life again in its basement quarters after its destruction and with its cinders still smoking above. The will to survive the Nazi period had its echoes in many stories told about homosexual life in the cities of Nazi Germany after the war.

Father, after becoming aware that my training toward a professional career in dance would take more than a year, announced to me that he would not be able to pay any more toward my training as a future *Hungerkünstler* (hunger artist). I left home after having been given a full scholarship, plus a small stipend toward board and food. As there was never enough to eat, my friend Gisela and I set out to compose a naughty dance, a dance we hoped to perform in the clubs that were frequented by British soldiers and their friends. After much trial and error, it turned out to be a pseudo-Apache dance with lots of throwing around, pushing, threatening, and stabbing gestures. We made the rather skimpy costumes ourselves, and, in a moment of inspiration, I decided that Gisela should wear a bra made of coarse fishnet, in which two bread rolls would make their own dance and out of which at the end I could take a lusty bite. It was a huge success, and our almost completely male audience shrieked and hollered with delight. We were always rewarded with a warm meal and several packs of English cigarettes, which we would sell on the black market. To satisfy our own desire for nicotine, we followed the soldiers with their fräuleins on the streets and in the parks to collect the discarded butts. Rolled in newspaper, they became perfectly acceptable smokes.

Despite the hardships, the almost one and a half years I spent as a student at the Folkwang School count among the happiest times of my life. From the very beginning, everything had its purpose, and I was training to learn a craft that would eventually, and I didn't realize how soon, lead me to become part of a theater family. It was my dream come true, and anything as unimportant as hardships of any kind could not put a damper on my good spirits and the happiness that signaled the beginning of a life in dance. My family, whom I had not visited for quite some time, never made any effort to contact me. Presuming that I would return at any moment to do penance and ask forgiveness for having abandoned common sense, they were waiting for my offer to step into Father's footsteps.

CHAPTER 9
Göttingen

In the summer of 1947, Gisela auditioned for a position with the Municipal Theater in Göttingen, was accepted, and consequently left the school. Meanwhile, Trude Pohl encouraged me to work on a number of my dances, which she planned to include in her next program. Out of the blue, I received an invitation to come to Göttingen for an audition, obviously the result of Gisela's suggestion. I recall my first reaction being one of anxiety. I was still inexperienced, devoid of a solid technique, but most importantly I had come to love the camaraderie at the school and waited several days before I decided to take the chance. I took the train on a Saturday morning, arriving in Göttingen at around noon. An open field and a dirt road separated the train station from the entrance to the city, which was still partially surrounded by a wall.

It was love at first sight when I set foot on the city streets. Göttingen, with its charming half-timbered houses, won my instant admiration, and I secretly hoped to be invited to dance there. An old city, Göttingen, reportedly dating back to 953 as the village of Gutingi, had received its town charter at the beginning of the thirteenth century. The war had avoided the city. It was the home of a famous university, whose creation in 1733 was made possible by the emperor Charles VI through the aid of George August of Hanover, who was also King George II of England. Many of the roofs of the buildings were marked with the signs of the Red Cross, warning approaching Allied Forces about the university's historical connections with the crown of England. Walking along the Theaterstrasse confirmed the very first impression I had experienced the moment I had entered the city, situated then very close to the border of Russian-occupied Germany. The street led me directly to the Theaterplatz and the Municipal Theater, renamed the Deutsches Theater since 1950 by its director Heinz Hilpert. But more about the director Hilpert later, as I worked for him after my years in Göttingen and before he took command of the theater there.

The beautiful theater, with its interior all dark red plush and gold ornamentation, had opened its doors in 1890. I entered via the stage door on the side of the building and, having been directed to the ballet studio on the second floor, I ran into my friend Gisela, who introduced me to the director-ballet master of the company. Otto Krüger, a very tall, very slim, and friendly man, made me feel welcome, and the reception by all the dancers in the studio gave me the confidence I so badly needed. My private audition was to be held several hours later in the presence of the feared and famous theater and opera director, a friend of Mary Wigman and Harald Kreutzberg: Hans Niedecken-Gebhard. At this first meeting with Gebhard, I had absolutely no clue as to who he was, but it didn't take me very long to experience the man's enormous gift as director, especially of operas by Handel, Purcell, Monteverdi, and other early composers, which he directed during the city's annual Handel Festivals, a tradition very much alive today and in which I participated at his request. Gebhard had the face of a bulldog, and he could snarl like one if he didn't get what he was after from a performer. He was the one who conducted the audition and seemed delighted when he saw that I could jump, spin, and glide through space at his command. In short, he gave me a one-hour workout that left me panting on the floor but resulted in a contract with the usual year-to-year term.

I had wanted to start work in the fall, so as to be able to dance on the program Trude Pohl had so generously offered me, but Niedecken-Gebhard had in mind that I should be dancing that summer in his upcoming production of *Dido and Aeneas* by Henry Purcell.

Returning to Essen-Werden, I had to confront my teacher, who, very upset and furious about my decision, begged me to stay. It was a painful confrontation, but I had signed a contract and was looking forward to being able to continue my training among male dancers and under a male teacher. It was, after all, Trude Pohl who had suggested that my future would be in the classical ballet area. I left with a heavy heart, leaving behind many friends, two of whom I would encounter again later on in life, and especially Trude Pohl, who followed my career with pride until her death in the late 1960s.

Back in Göttingen, I had a few days to deal with official business, like a personal appearance at the police headquarters to register as a newly arrived resident, after which I was allowed to search for a room in which to live. Times were at their worst in postwar Germany, food rationing at its strictest, and obviously a dancer's salary was not meant to be spent at the black market. Although as professional dancers we received extra food rations, just as coal miners did, it just never seemed to be enough. Once a week, I stood in line to receive the weekly allowance: one loaf of bread of the cottony variety, so unlike the prewar German bread. It could easily be consumed in a few bites, which, of course, I always did.

On the other hand, I was busy taking classes, rehearsing the dances for *Dido and Aeneas*, and making new friends in the process. I had found a room in an old house that was part of a unified street frontage dating back to the sixteenth century. All the way at the

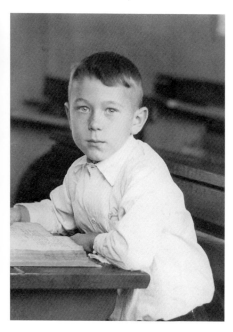

Left Heinz as a young boy in school-room, undated.

Right Heinz at First Communion with his mother, undated.

Right At military training camp in Denmark, 1943.

Below Heinz in naval uniform, circa 1944.

Left In Germany, 1946.

Below Hans Werner Henze, Heinz's apartment in Gottingen, 1948.

Heinz at the Berlin Zoo, 1949.

Heinz in *Don Juan*, National Ballet of Chile, undated.

Heinz in *Sleeping Beauty*, National Ballet of Chile, undated.

Heinz as Standard Bearer in National Ballet of Chile's performance of *The Green Table*, 1956.

Left Heinz in Chile, 1962.

Right In Chile, before leaving for Paris, 1962.

top, five rickety flights up, was the small room that I rented from an old lady. It contained a box spring with a mattress, a bowl on a stand with a bucket of water at its side, and a chair on which stood a small lamp. The only toilet for all the tenants in the house was somewhere downstairs in the backyard, an outhouse I never used, always taking care of such business late at night in the theater and at arrival in the morning, adding the use of the shower to my daily luxury.

As a dancer I progressed very quickly. The dances Krüger choreographed for *Dido and Aeneas*, mainly dances for men carrying shields and spears, were difficult and exhausting. But I loved the music and didn't mind a bit repeating the same dance phrase over and over. Krüger's method for composing dances was orderly and predictable. Knowing his score by heart, and having predetermined the steps and choreographic patterns, he never introduced any surprise in his work. But, as time went on, he eventually involved a few of us in his creative process. There was, of course, Gisela, a very intuitive mover, who was not afraid to argue when something felt awkward or just plain wrong, and Kurt Paudler, a highly individualistic and mature dancer. He also had been trained at the Wigman School and already had had a career as a solo dancer. My contribution could only have been minimal, although I had a very good ear for music and automatically righted any glitch that sprang from the choreography. Krüger actually encouraged the three of us to comment should some fault come to our attention during work on a ballet. He believed in teamwork, which led him to invite us often to his home, where, over dinner prepared by his wife Ursula, also a dancer in our company, we would discuss the day's work.

One evening each week at the theater, usually Wednesdays, was called *Ballettabend* (ballet evening). All other days were given to operas, operettas, and plays. Operas and operettas demanded dances and dancers, and so new and different styles had to be learned, frequently and quickly. With *Carmen* on the roster of operas, we were taught by a Spanish dance teacher to play the castanets and do pseudo Spanish dances, while waltzing was an absolute must for the annual New Year's Eve presentation of *Die Fledermaus*.

The variety of operas and operettas we danced in was staggering, and, thanks to Fritz Lehman, the theater's *Intendant* (theater director) and principal conductor, production values were very high in every department. Himself a first-class conductor, Lehman possessed impeccable taste and was considered advanced for the time because of his adventurous programming. He made it a point to conduct all ballet performances himself. Perhaps it was the choice of music for our ballets that provided him with the stimulus for his involvement with our productions. I do not recall him conducting operettas, except perhaps *Die Fledermaus* on New Year's Eve, but he was, without exception, involved in every production during the month long Handel Festivals.

Needless to say, Niedecken-Gebhard's masterful stagings and directions of Purcell's *Dido and Aeneas* and Handel's *Terpsichore* and *Ariadne auf Naxos*, to be followed by Purcell's *The Fairy Queen* and Monteverdi's *Orfeo* and *Il Ballo delle Ingrate*, some of them of considerable length, made the time of performance fly. As a featured dancer in his productions, I learned and became very much influenced by his extraordinary discipline and respect for his art. He had the admiration of all involved: singers, dancers, and technicians alike.

My first major assignment came with Krüger's announcement that I was to dance Prince Ivan in Stravinsky's *Firebird*. It was to be my introduction to the city's ballet audience, and we worked feverishly for many weeks towards its completion. My costume, a tailored brocade jacket and heavy silk Cossack pants with a pair of red boots, gave my appearance a decidedly princely look, and I eagerly anticipated opening night. The set for the first scene represented an enchanted garden, divided from the rest of the world by a ten-foot-high wall, onto which I had to climb from behind with the help of a ladder. From the top, I would surprise a princess and her consort engaged in play with golden balls to the mysterious strains of Stravinsky's music. Armed with bow and arrow, I made my gradual appearance before an expectant and hushed audience, which led to chaos and consternation among the ball-playing entourage, who scurried in every direction at the moment I jumped the ten feet onto the stage.

As instructed, I landed crouched with bow and arrow poised, when I noticed that my tensed stomach muscles had broken the cord that held up my heavy silk pants. As my jacket had been fitted very snugly around my waist and I was to exit again very soon, and in the hope that the tight fit would hold my pants up for the duration of that time, I dared to straighten up. My pants fell to my ankles, leaving me poised, with bow and arrow, in my dance belt. Pandemonium broke out, and the curtain came down. I was utterly devastated and probably the only one backstage, except for the wardrobe mistress, not on the verge of breaking up with laughter. In the end, the wardrobe mistress was held responsible for using a cord instead of the usual inch-wide rubber band for dancers' costumes. I, not yet experienced in such matters, had simply overlooked that fact.

After that mistake had been corrected behind the scenes and Fritz Lehman had commenced once more at the beginning of the score, the curtain was raised again, revealing the ball-playing scene. My appearance on top of the wall was greeted with applause until the moment of that infamous jump when the audience shrieked and hooted until I again straightened up, only this time with pants in place, to thunderous applause. Most performing artists experience at least once during their careers some sort of embarrassing mishap, but to this day I believe that my unfortunate situation on that so important day of my first appearance as a solo dancer deserves to be shared, and the humorous aspect of it to be enjoyed by all. It testifies to the frailness of everyone involved in the performing arts, but also to the glory of our profession. To witness how performers overcome moments of darkness during a performance is also to see that we are human: skilled, yes, but nonetheless human and not gods.

At the end, the ballet proved successful with our first-night audience, and the press lauded the production the following day. My personal mishap, although revealed in detail, did not overshadow the rest of my performance. Opening night parties at the time were usually avoided because the lack of food and drink rendered such gatherings pointless. What made those nights special was the anticipation of audience approval. The lesson I learned from that night was that dancers' costumes should always be made to move with the dancer, an ideal hardly ever realized on a first night, unless the dance has had the luxury of a long gestation period with costumes in place. This reminds me of the perfect harmony arrived at by Kreutzberg, who had designed and constructed his own costumes and perhaps had created his dances around and in them.

Accompanied by these and other thoughts about my performance that night, I went home to prepare my late supper. My landlady had graciously encouraged me to make use of a small, two-burner cooking device she kept in her kitchen. All I had left was some grits and a few raisins. Thrown together and cooked in water, it thickened into gruel. The only setback was the cold. My room had no heat, and the water in the bucket had frozen, so I consumed the food in bed under the blanket, before falling asleep. Eventually, I found a very charming living space in a building across the street from the old town hall that housed a bridal store on the second floor, run by the owner of the building and her daughter.

Frau Kahler, a smallish chubby woman in her sixties, was in love with the theater. Her apartment occupied the entire third floor, with me making my new home another flight up at the top of the building. A little anteroom, equipped with a large stone sink, led to an ample room with a window overlooking the rooftops of near and faraway houses and the hilly landscapes that surrounded the city. A mattress in one corner on the floor, a narrow armoire, a table on which stood a small gasoline-fueled stove with two burn-ers, and several chairs comprised the inventory. Frau Kahler lent me the necessary utensils, plates, and coffee cups. She had a son, whom I never met, who lived in another town. I somehow replaced that son for her; she lavished her motherly attention on me whenever the opportunity arose, usually whenever I climbed the stairs to my room. She would call after me to inquire if I had eaten or if I had enough food. She always had something to give, something she had made. I even had permission to use her indoor toilet, the only other one being an outhouse on the landing, except, of course, during the night, when I would pee in the stone sink in my anteroom.

In time I made more friends. Besides Gisela and Kurt Paudler, there was another Kurt, the character actor Kurt A. Jung, who had just made his successful debut in the comedy *Three Men on a Horse*. And then there was Susanne, daughter of Fritz Lehman, who had made the move from Zürich to Göttingen, to be close to her parents. Susanne was a brilliant actress and seductive to the point that made us lovers, if only for a short time. We did, however, spend some anx-ious time together while waiting for Susi's belated period to occur. Needless to say, we were overjoyed to have escaped unwanted par-enthood, and we are still best friends to this day. I will always remem-ber her in the title role of Anouilh's *Eurydice*, but especially as Jenny in *The Beggar's Opera*, that forerunner of *The Three-Penny Opera*, and as the maid in Thornton Wilder's *The Skin of Our Teeth*.

We all loved spending time together, usually in discussion about the plays, ballets, or operas being performed, but mostly just to have fun together. Those were the times when everyone, contributing one potato, cooked and made into a salad, thought of it as an extraordinary event.

I tend to think sometimes that life was easier then, with our youth playing an important role in that perception. There was nothing to distract us from our total commitment to our respective chosen professions: no TV, an occasional movie, otherwise just books, radio, and a record player, if you could afford and find one. Our country's horrendous recent past was still too undisclosed for us to grasp its monumental importance. That reality would soon cast its shadows over our land. Our worries included such mundane things as washing and ironing our clothes, an almost daily necessity, considering the fact that one change of clothes was all most of us had. Our days were divided between the constant search for food and drink, dancing, rehearsing, and sleeping, and starting that search for food again the following day. Yes, at that particular time life seemed easier, simpler, and much less complicated; we were young, we didn't possess anything, and, therefore, we had nothing to lose.

It was at that time that I would experience a strangely disturbing incident, occurring during a performance by the visiting and to me unknown solo dancer, Dore Hoyer. What I thought would be a fun evening of dance became much more serious as I watched this solo dancer perform with austere and remarkable strength the cycle of five of her dances which she titled *Der Grosse Gesang* (The Great Song). The cycle opened and closed with *Tanz der göttlichen Besessenheit* (Dance of the Divine Possession). One has to have seen Dore Hoyer dance to comprehend the immense impact she exerted on me and many others. As soon as she had begun the last dance, a repeat performance of the first dance, I broke down. Unable to control my sobbing, surrounded by Susanne and Kurt Paudler, I had become oblivious to what was going on around me. When the theater had emptied, my friends were finally able to get me home, where I spent two consecutive days staring into space. I guess that nowadays such a state of mind would be equated with a temporary nervous breakdown.

Hoyer was all that makes some great artists produce emotions that remain unexplainable to us lesser mortals. Although she had been a student of Palucca and Wigman, it must have been the demon in her that had produced her astounding technique that seemed to have no boundaries of expression. On stage she was a rebel, a prosecutor, and always a revolutionary. She reminded me of a huge mass of granite, always poised to plunge down on whatever was in her way. With her pianist Dimitri Wiatowitsch, she created dances that pierced the space around her. With analytical clarity and sharpness, she always challenged and provoked writers, painters, and other artists. The greater public had by now been lured by Ulanova, Plissetskaya, the Royal Ballet, Roland Petit, and, of course, Balanchine. Hoyer committed suicide on New Year's Eve 1967–68 (at the age of fifty-six), only days before she was to be honored with the German Kritiker Preis, an award which would have brought her name to the public in a way that her solo dancing had not been able to accomplish.

I met Dore Hoyer on several occasions. When she was ballet mistress at the Hamburg State Opera in the early 1950s, I made the trip from Berlin to attend an audition she was holding. Her appointment at the opera caused some consternation among the other important and classically oriented ensembles at the German state-supported theaters. Although she had confessed her admiration for "good toe dancing," Hoyer's work at the Hamburg State Opera did not satisfy the city's conservative audience, and eventually they parted company. While I had, unsuccessfully, auditioned for her, I also attended one of her classes.

Alone on the stage, she symbolized what could be defined as genius, as she would demonstrate again during her performances in Santiago, Chile, during my tenure there with the National Ballet. While a guest at the home of Ernst Uthoff and Lola Botka, founders of the Chilean National Ballet, I found her aloof and mysterious. She seemed to be part of a different world, a different life, only an encapsulation of her art.

In 1983, I choreographed a dance that was meant to reflect my image of Dore Hoyer. Ellen Kogan, a modern dancer I had met and seen in performance at the Jacob's Pillow Dance Festival in Beckett, Massachusetts, would eventually become the perfect talent for my ambitious undertaking. Ellen turned out to be a dancer possessed. It was only thanks to her indefatigable strength and willingness to search for the truth in the choreography that we succeeded. *Tristeza* would evolve as a perfect vehicle for Ellen as a solo artist.

Back at the theater in Göttingen, we were at work for the next ballet, Manuel de Falla's *Three-Cornered Hat*. I landed the role of the *Bürgermeister* (mayor), a part I loathed. Apart from the music, I found the ballet silly and hoped for something more substantial to come my way soon.

We ended our season, and rehearsals for the Handel Festival would begin soon. After discovering that I wasn't needed for the first part of the festival, I accepted an invitation to dance in Mozart's *Marriage of Figaro* in one of the small German towns whose names are preceded by the word *Bad* (Bath). These places are the favorite destinations for the imaginary ill, drinking bad-smelling waters in the hope of a cure from intestinal and other ailments. Much money and time is spent on mud and sulfur baths, rest, and food, but also on *Kultur* (culture).

Not very far from Göttingen, in this pretty little town whose name has escaped me, I met Hans Werner Henze. Hans Werner had been a student of the composer Wolfgang Fortner and was himself in the process of making music that would soon be heard in Europe's concert halls. For now he had been engaged as conductor of the Mozart opera. We became lovers, and it took me very little time to convince him to come with me to Göttingen, where I was sure he would be overwhelmed by the quality of the festival. Thoroughly impressed after the conclusion of the festival, Hans Werner rented a baby grand piano, to the delight of Frau Kahler, who hoped the house would always be filled with music. It was in this room on Weender Strasse 20 that Hans Werner composed part of his first two symphonies and a number of other, smaller compositions. He had given me a few lessons on the piano and, once, when he was out of town on a conducting assignment, my attempt at composing a small one-page composition became a teaching tool for Fortner's students at his home in Heidelberg. However, the study of piano never took roots with me, as it was my feet and legs that aspired to artistic expression.

In the ballet *Kirmes von Delft* (Kermess in Delft) by Hermann Reutter, the role of the devil had me dance with a boot on one foot and a toe shoe on the other. I had to experiment for quite some time to see which of my feet would more successfully manipulate the tricky choreography on that one shoe. The foot with the boot seemed to be constantly in the way, but we were finally able to unravel a complex choreographic process with our customary tenacity. The slave in the ballet *Scheherazade* became perhaps my best part at that time, although, thinking back, the choreography must have been simplistic by today's standards. I much preferred a solo I danced in the ballet *Der Dämon* (The Demon) by Hindemith, and a part in Rimsky-Korsakov's *Capriccio Espanol*.

During much of our free time, we worked on solo dances, which we eventually assembled into a cohesive whole that took the shape of a *Tanz Abend* (Evening of Dance) with soloists from the Municipal Theater of Göttingen. For the occasion, Hans Werner composed a dance for me that presented a real challenge that I was finally able to translate into a sort of machine-dance and which turned out to be a novelty on our program.

But the time came when I felt that I had to move on and to be faced with greater challenges. I auditioned and signed a contract with the Stuttgart Ballet, for the 1948 season, long before John Cranko took over the company and rebuilt it into a major force in ballet. Meanwhile, Hans Werner had been contracted by Heinz Hilpert as conductor for the newly formed Deutsches Theater in Konstanz am Bodensee on the Swiss border. Hilpert had also engaged Marcel Luipart, who had been a member of the Ballet Russe de Monte Carlo, to assemble a small group of dancers to become part of his theatrical experiments. Henze, anticipating an exciting new venture, urged me to audition. The offer to join the group left me with the problem of already having committed myself to Stuttgart. After some friendly intervention by Hilpert and Henze, and after having found a substitute, I was released from my obligation to the Stuttgart Ballet and free to join the Deutsches Theater in Konstanz am Bodensee.

CHAPTER 10
Konstanz

The shortness of my stay in Konstanz, from 1949 until January 1950, was due to financial problems. The city had to deal with the fact that the recent devaluation of the German currency had given every citizen forty new German marks. This had made all the money we had in our possession useless. The magnitude of it did not really sink in until the following day when we discovered the availability of everything we had lacked for so many years. There were foodstuffs in all their former glory, clothing we had only dreamed of, and all of it accessible if you had the money to buy it. My forty marks had to last until the end of that month, and it became necessary at first to figure out how much to spend per day while gathering information about the cost of those luxuries. Of course, I spent much more than I should have, and after two weeks it meant pressing my nose against shop windows, daydreaming. But we all survived, adjusting and learning to live a new way of life, a life we had forgotten but recaptured with amazing speed. Word spread soon that money for our salaries had become unavailable, which led finally to the demise of our group. As irony would have it, not long afterward the Municipal Theater in Göttingen changed its name to Deutsches Theater with Hilpert as its leader.

The six months in Konstanz are crammed with memories. I grew as a dancer under Luipart, matured as a person, and learned more about the theater and its discipline than I would have anywhere else. Heinz Hilpert was a man of the theater, with his sensibilities extending to music, especially Bach and Mozart, whom he referred to as God and Jesus Christ. He loved classical dance, which he always described to his actors as the most revealing of human nature. While he directed Goethe's *Egmont,* I spent much of my time sitting by his side, listening to his instructions, his reprimands, and encouragements. He pointed out to me the subtleties of pronunciation, which he would test from every part of the theater. It was not uncommon for him to cancel an opening because an actor failed to project a whispered word to the last row in the balcony. His adaptation of Schiller's *Mary Stuart,* which he cut to approximately an hour and a half, with a young, twenty-three-year-old actress in the role of Elizabeth, resulted in an exciting, James Bond-like version of the overlong play. Brilliant at directing comedy and drama alike, Hilpert was a visionary, integrating music and dance into his work, just as Max Reinhardt, for whom he had worked as assistant and actor, had done.

Hans Werner was busy rehearsing the orchestra for the opening of *Egmont.* We both had become close, as other members of the cast had, to Nuschka, Hilpert's wife. During the war, while Hilpert was working in Berlin and Vienna, Nuschka, because she was a Jew, had been planning to escape to Switzerland. After a long and torturous journey, she made it to their Swiss friends, where she spent the rest of the war. We all loved her generosity and spirit. Before the devaluation of the German mark, food was still very scarce, but Nuschka always seemed to find ways to prepare a meal for us. We all lived in the same hotel, and Hilpert himself, when not in the theater, could only be found in bed. Here he received his visitors, among whom we counted famous German film and theater actors, men and woman who owed their fame to him and who momentarily would shed their studied image of themselves. I observed that their greetings at times consisted of locking their little fingers together. After pulling them apart, the resulting farts would make them explode with laughter. Only many years later did I learn that Hilpert had been sent with Joachim von Ribbentropp to Paris to convince Marlene Dietrich to return to the Reich. However, history records Dietrich's refusal and her subsequent decision to apply for American citizenship.

Marcel Luipart, himself an excellent dancer, had hired three female dancers for our small ensemble of five. Once a week, we presented our own *Tanzabend*, which had become part of the normal playbill. Jutta Brintz, my Sylphide, ended up married to an American soldier and later moved to America. Still my friend and living in California, she has managed to keep our friendship alive for over fifty years.

Perhaps due to our youth, the passionate affair Hans Werner and I shared for two years came to an emotional end in Berlin shortly after my arrival. We had loved each other deeply and on one occasion tried to mend what had been broken. I always knew about his enormous talent during those years of our friendship and always labeled him as a "new romantic." Hans Werner is very famous now, and I continue to love his music and admire his talent very much.

Berlin

After Hans Werner had left for Berlin, I received an invitation from Tatjana Gsovsky, who was in charge of the ballet company at the Berlin State Opera, to appear for an audition. As I didn't have the money for a train trip to Berlin, Tatjana telegraphed the money to me. A high-level fear befell all passengers traveling through Russian-occupied Germany. Rumors about the confiscation of identity papers, or of people not being allowed to board the train again after being searched by border guards made the trip an uncomfortable experience. At the border inspection proper, all of our papers were collected and taken inside a building. After an interminable wait, we finally got our identification back, under the suspicious glance of a Russian officer.

After our arrival at the station Berlin am Zoo, I walked the short distance to Tatjana's home on Fasanenstrasse 68, just off the Kurfürstendamm, in the British-occupied sector of the city. Berlin was still gray and much of it in ruins but mostly cleared of debris. But there was life. After a few weeks, I even thought I detected some of the famous atmosphere that gave Berlin before Hitler the reputation for divine depravity. The many cabarets and innumerable nightclubs, gay and straight or often both, the numerous theaters, many in improvised venues and full of vitality and invention, were a trait Berliners share with New Yorkers, as I would experience later.

Tatjana hired me and found my feet especially expressive. It was not the custom in Germany to be hired in midseason, but I signed a contract that would have me start work in three months. Meanwhile, the Friederichstadt Palast, a very large variety theater with its own ballet company, hired me as its lead dancer, replacing Gert Reinholm, Tatjana's protégé and star dancer at the State Opera. I myself would become the star in a ballet titled *Der Abenteurer von Venedig* (The Adventurer from Venice), set to Tchaikovsky's *Italian Serenade*, with choreography by Jans Keith. The ballet was a free adaptation of Boccaccio's love affairs. With a cast of twelve and a large corps de ballet, it was the most populated ballet I had ever danced in. The scenery, with its bridges over running water, suggestive of Venice at night, was almost alone worth the price of admission. The theater seated approximately three thousand, and the house seemed to be filled every day, which turned out to be of great benefit for me prior to joining the Berlin State Opera as a soloist. For three months, every day and twice on Saturdays and Sundays, I made love to Gisela Deege, Sigrid Hary, Valivia, and Edel von Rothe.

Berlin had become my new love. Despite the fact that the city was divided into four sectors, it pulsed, except in the gray and bleak Soviet-occupied sector. Berlin had survived the Russian siege, and the wall was still in the not-too-near future. The original State Opera House on Unter den Linden had been bombed, and its temporary substitute, that venerable old Metropol Theater, served as the home for opera and ballet. The Komische Oper, also in the Russian sector, was operating successfully under the leadership of Felsenstein, as was the Deutsches Schauspielhaus where Bertolt Brecht reigned.

The U-Bahn station on the Friederichstrasse was my daily point of arrival, which led me to the nearby Friederichstadt Palast. Now, as a member of the State Opera Ballet, I just crossed the street to enter the portal of the Metropol Theater and my own dressing room. The attention lavished on us dancers was astounding. A massage after every class and before the performance was a daily ritual. A personal dresser and all-around admirer servant, plus the makeup man, were constant followers, awaiting my exit from the stage to dry my sweaty face and nurture my growing vanity. Besides Gert Reinholm, Gisela Deege, and Edel von Rothe, there was the excellent Peter van Dijk. Rainer Köcherman, Denise Laumer, Giselle Vesco, and Maria Fries completed the roster of soloists, headed by Natascha Trofimova as its female star. Maria Fries, several years later, committed suicide by throwing herself onto the stage from the flyspace above. Maria's complex had always been about her size. She was very small, an exceptional technician and all-around beautiful dancer who dreamed of having the height and long legs of a Balanchine dancer. We were friends, but she was in constant need of assurances that her height was of no importance.

Personally, I had made dramatic improvements in class and on the stage, which resulted in my being assigned to take over for an injured Reinholm, in the leading male role in *Dornröschen* (The Sleeping Beauty), with choreography by Tatjana, after Petipa. Natascha, a very strong and beautiful dancer, had scared me to death by announcing after my assignment: "Well, let's see if he can handle me." A first rehearsal met with her approval, and we soon melted into each other's arms. At one performance, Rainer Köcherman had suddenly taken ill, which required that I change costume and dance the Bluebird pas de deux in addition to my role as the prince. Never would I have said no to any assignment. My stamina had no limits, and I wanted to do it all. Another major role I danced in Tatjana's staging of *Don Quixote* became my favorite part. It was a beautiful pas de deux with Denise Laumer, abstract in character and original in its use of ballet technique.

Prince Charming had never been my favorite role. I threw myself into it to prove that I could do it, but with no great enthusiasm. Somehow I had always defined dance to be sufficient unto itself, like the solos I had created at the Folkwang School and the dances I had seen in films by Fred Astaire. In short, it was just the music and my reaction to it that mattered. If there was a story, it would have to be exclusively in the mind of the beholder. Stories were to be read; it was that simple for me, and I grew more and more disenchanted with the idea of having to act princely roles for the rest of my career as a dancer. Acting was something I had wanted to do years ago, when all I had aspired to was to go on-stage. Now fate had led me into a career in dance, something I had already done subconsciously while skating. It was now fate again when the New York City Ballet came to Berlin and opened its program with *Concerto Barocco*. Those twenty minutes changed my life; dance won out. From then on, I became aware of the many possibilities inherent in classical ballet vocabulary that would for me become the touchstone on how to perceive dance and its relationship to music.

Very soon after my arrival in Berlin, I had received an offer to join the National Ballet of Chile from its founder and director, Ernst Uthoff. Uthoff had been an important member of the Ballet Jooss. Kurt Jooss, whom I had met at the Folkwang School when I was a student there, eventually had to disband his company while on tour in the Americas. Three of its dancers—Uthoff, his wife Lola Botka, and Rudolf Pescht—had returned to Chile at the invitation of the Chilean government, to open a school and eventually form a company.

Its beginnings in 1942 would result in Jooss himself staging his signature works: *Big City*, *Pavanne for a Dead Infanta*, *A Ball in Old Vienna*, and his great masterwork, *The Green Table*. All of the above were unknown to me when I received the invitation to come to Chile. Where was Chile? After having consulted a world atlas, I decided that it was at the end of the world. Playing for time, I wired back that a knee injury prevented me from immediately accept-ing the invitation. In truth, I was expecting Tatjana's return from Buenos Aires, where she was staging her ballet *Juan de Zarissa* at the Teatro Colón. I needed her advice about a part of the world of which I knew nothing. At her return, she told me that she had met Uthoff in Buenos Aires and that, yes, the National Ballet of Chile was one of the most reputable companies in that part of the world.

Shortly after, I received a letter from Trude Pohl about Uthoff. He had recently been in England and Germany searching for a dancer, and she, his former colleague in the Ballet Jooss, had told him to hire me sight unseen. She knew I was in Berlin and had given him my address, and so I found myself wanted, but unsure about a move so far from home. At the same time, I tried to come to terms with the difficulty of leaving Berlin, so I decided momentarily to forget about it. But an unforeseen incident would change my life for me.

Tatjana had left a woman in charge whom nobody had ever seen or heard about. All we knew was that she had been a dancer, been injured, and been left with a limp. A few of us who lived in the west sector suspected that Tatjana had been pressured by the Soviet authorities to let herself be temporarily replaced by this woman. Many of the communist bosses had repeatedly complained about Tatjana's use of non-Russian music.

Lunchtime every Saturday was the occasion for political indoc-trination to be held in the auditorium for all musicians, singers, and dancers. Attendance was obligatory and resulted mostly in many of us just munching an apple, eating a sandwich, and barely understand-ing what was being said and discussed at the front of the house. On one of those Saturdays, after our morning class had ended, the lady in question, whose name I do not remember, reminded us about the importance of the meeting to be held in half an hour, which elicited from me a clear and loud expletive in response. I momentarily had forgotten where I was, but a whispered "Get out, I don't like how she looked at you" from a colleague, brought me back to reality.

Pretending to look casual, I nonetheless hurried to my dressing room. Grabbing my coat and dance bag, I ran toward the exit door in my slippers. However, to reach the door, one needed to cross the stage on the side where the stage manager resides during performances and where the only phone was located. In the semidarkness, and just as I reached the exit door, I heard her voice: "He's just leaving." Fortunately for me, the S-Bahn station is across the street. To get to the station, I had to push myself through the marching Communist Youth rally currently under way in Berlin. I caught the departing train in time, arriving safely at the next station in the west sector.

Changing into my shoes and getting home as soon as possible was all I could think about. It was winter and very cold. Tatjana's cook and all-around helper, a wonderful older woman who took care of me, was home. After I confided to her what had happened, she reminded me that it would not be wise for me to venture out on the street, where undesirables in the Soviets' view were often pulled into cars in the western sectors, not to be heard from again. It also didn't take long before the *Intendant*, the theater's manager, who himself lived in the British sector, called to let me know that the Russian police had indeed shown up at the theater inquiring about my whereabouts.

That same day I found refuge with good friends, the Ramas, then well-known photographers in Berlin, who lived around the corner on the Kurfürstendamm in a spacious apartment on the fifth floor. Only Tatjana's helper knew about my hiding place, where she would deliver any mail addressed to me. It was she who ultimately brought the telegram from Chile asking about the condition of my knee and offering me a contract in case I was able to dance. The return answer was paid for. All I had to do was say the word "yes" and my plane ticket would be on its way. Everybody's reaction, including my own, was obvious. The sooner I left Berlin, the better for me, and so I cabled my answer immediately.

The only obstacle now was to obtain a passport so I could leave the country, which my friends the Ramas solved by accompanying me in a taxi to the British Embassy. Here I told my story, and, after presenting my contract, I was assured that with plane ticket in hand, a passport to leave Germany would be mine. It took less than a week for the ticket to arrive, with reservations made for a stopover in Frankfurt, where I needed to get a visa from the Chilean Embassy. From there, a BOAC plane would take me to London, where a change of planes would take me to Santiago, Chile. A few other minor official German bureaucratic visits had to be taken care of, where I learned that only forty German marks could be taken out of the country.

As the day of my departure drew close, I grew sadder and sadder at the thought of having to leave Berlin and my friends behind. At the Berlin Tempelhof Airport, after having checked my small and only suitcase, a loan from the Ramas, I cried, my friends cried, and people around us cried until I was urged to enter the plane. As far as all my other friends and family were concerned, I simply vanished.

CHAPTER 12

The Journey

I left Berlin during the second half of December 1951. My trip should have lasted two days, but endless delays would prolong the journey for a whole week. Planes still had propellers, and it was not uncommon for one of them to stop working or to start smoking. Such mishaps had to be taken care of in the form of unscheduled landings. The airlines were extremely generous in those days, rewarding their passengers with the best hotel accommodations, the best food and drink, free taxi rides, and chocolates, liquor and cigarettes galore. Actually, on that trip to Chile, we passengers became almost a family.

But I must return to the beginning of that journey. After landing in Frankfurt, I made my way to the Chilean Embassy, where my forty German marks shrank to just four after I paid thirty-six marks for my visa. Someone drove me back to the airport, where I boarded the flight to London, and where another transfer would carry me to my scheduled destination. On that flight I found myself the only passenger, and it was explained to me that this flight was for diplomats only, except that no diplomat was flying on that day. A passport from the British authorities in Berlin must have given me special consideration for travel outside of Germany, which was still not easy or common. My knowledge of the English language was practically nonexistent, and the crew on board, speaking only rudimentary German, made me aware that landing in London was impossible because of excessive fog. Our destination became a mystery for me.

After we had landed (and I still do not have a clue as to where that was), I passed inspection with flying colors because of my few and used possessions. But after it was revealed that only four German marks would have to keep me alive for my journey to South America, the officials stared at me in total disbelief. In the midst of their hilarity, they waved me through. In fact, my explanation about a job in Chile had missed its point because of our language barrier.

It was now late and dark, but someone pointed me in the direction of a number of low buildings. When I entered one of them, it became clear that many planes destined for London had landed here, because the place was packed with people, stranded like me. At one point, an announcement was made over several loudspeakers, of which I didn't understand a word. Everybody proceeded to exit, toward a long row of what looked to me like taxicabs. What else was I to do but follow, boarding one of the cars that were soon filled, holding my little suitcase on my lap. Among the other passengers, several languages were spoken but unmistakably no German. It began to dawn on me that, because Germany had lost the war and had been the aggressor, I should conceal my identity and keep myself inconspicuous.

We finally arrived at a large hotel. After leaving the taxicabs, we entered the hotel and stood in long lines. Anticipating the inevitable when my turn at the desk would come, I experienced extreme discomfort, which I tried to calm with the knowledge that I possessed a plane ticket. Having handed over passport and ticket, I inquired in German if somebody spoke my language. I was curtly told "no," a word I understood. But at that moment I felt someone touching my shoulder, and a man's voice announced to me that he spoke German and that he could handle my affairs at the desk for me. A very well-dressed gentleman in his early fifties, he was, as I would learn later, a British diplomat arriving from a vacation in Spain with his wife, an invalid. When handing me the key to my room, he instructed me to join him and his wife for breakfast at 7:00 A.M. the next morning.

Of course, I hardly slept that night. The room was very cold, and I didn't have any English coins to feed the heater in the wall. I crawled into bed in my clothes because it was too cold to get undressed. Counting the hours, I waited for the day to break. It was still dark when I finally jumped out of bed. In my overcoat, I waited until my watch had turned to 7:00 A.M. Descending the stairs, I spotted the couple already sitting in the large dining room. After I had introduced myself to the wife, a youngish and pretty woman in a wheelchair who spoke German, the breakfast selections were displayed on the table. After being provided with coffee and tea, we consumed the most substantial morning meal I had ever eaten. I hardly had a chance to speak because my benefactors conversed exclusively in English.

Breakfast over, the gentleman paid the bill and informed me that a taxicab would soon take us to the train station where we would board the train to London. When after a lengthy trip we had arrived in London, he instructed a taxi driver about which route to take, so I would be able to see some of the most important sights of the city and to make a stop at the airport. His wife, who translated his instructions to me, commented about all the historical sights we passed. At the airport, he personally arranged for my flight that evening.

Our tour ended at the couple's large apartment on the second floor of a large building. The furniture in the apartment had been covered with white bed sheets, the removal of which was followed by the preparation of a late lunch. When my time had come to leave, the gentleman called a taxicab and handed me the money to pay the driver. We simply said good-bye. In conversation, they had made it clear that I didn't need to thank them. There was no exchange of addresses, and I didn't even learn their names. Even though they knew my name from my passport, they never uttered it. It was like a dream. I have often wondered what might have happened to me, stranded in a foreign country, at the wrong airport and with only four German marks in my pocket, without their help. I always was and still am profoundly grateful to those nameless people who had made it a point to help another person in need.

The plane, its final destination Santiago, Chile, was packed with the most gorgeous-looking black people, mostly very tall women, some of them with their babies, who wore their colorful, festive garments with amazing grace and panache. There were men, too, tall, strong, and bold in appearance. They all seemed to me to come from another planet. When we left the plane at our first unscheduled stop, somewhere in Portugal, I encountered the same tall, handsome people, in charge of transporting us and our luggage to a most luxurious exotic hotel among huge palm trees on the oceanfront. Here we were feted, buffet-style, with every delicacy one could think of. Most of them I had never seen, tasted, or even heard of. And then there was champagne, lots of it, and we all indulged until shortly before midnight, when we finally bade each other good night.

At the reasonable hour of 8:00 A.M., we ate a copious breakfast, including some strange and exotic fruit, after which we were transported again to board the repaired plane that took us to the first scheduled stop in Dakar, West Africa. After lunch, we crossed the Atlantic to land in Halifax, Nova Scotia, and on to Nassau, capital of the Bahama Islands. Here we spent the night. I remember my enormous hotel room, with three large open spaces for windows facing the street below. After assurances from the management that it was perfectly safe to fall asleep, I went to bed.

Our next stop in Kingston, the capital of Jamaica, was also unscheduled. After having been served lunch, we spent the rest of a very hot day drinking rum mixed with pineapple juice. In total stupor and after having eaten another hearty meal, we departed late in the evening. The number of passengers had shrunk by now to something like twenty-five, since all the black people had disembarked in either Nassau or Kingston. By now we had crossed the language barrier with gestures and a few sentences we had taught each other.

The constant supply of food and drink on and off the plane made us swear to go on a fast after our arrival in Panama City, our next landing site. We then fantasized about what we would eat after our fast when in Lima, Peru, our last stop before landing in Santiago de Chile. Everybody on the plane took part in the game of concocting elaborate menus for our arrival in Lima. Even the stewardesses participated.

The menus were passed around to great hilarity, corrected and changed by passengers who professed to know better which wine to serve with lobster, for example. Unfortunately, our stopover in Lima turned out to be the shortest on the whole trip, only a little more than an hour, but most had already broken the promise of fasting in Panama City. Only a handful of us had avoided food until our landing in Peru. An announcement had made it clear that Lima was going to be a no-no for a gorging fiesta.

Finally, the last stretch from Lima to Santiago came to its conclusion. Below, we could see the city, surrounded partially by the Andes. Perhaps fifteen of us were left on the plane, and we had already said good-bye to each other after having spent more than a week in proximity on that small, propeller-driven plane. I looked down at the city, so far from my homeland, never imagining that it would be ten years before I would leave Chile.

On arrival, I was greeted by Ernst Uthoff, founder and director of the Chilean National Ballet, his wife Lola Botka, teacher and dancer with the company, and Rudolf Pescht, who had also been a major figure of the Ballet Jooss. Pescht had retired from dancing but was still working as an important coach of the roles he had danced in the Jooss repertory. Then there was Patricio Bunster, who had been one of the first dancers since the company's inception in 1942. Patricio would in later years join Uthoff as associate director and choreographer. After introductions and greetings, the Uthoffs took me to their home, where we got better acquainted with each other over lunch. It was summer in Chile. The warmth and brilliant sunshine exerted its charm on me. For now, a small, temporary apartment had been rented for me downtown, and I was given some local currency to hold me over until my first payday in January. As members of the National Ballet, we were like the Symphony Orchestra, the Choir, and the Teatro Experimental, public employees who enjoyed exemplary benefits, administered through the Extension Musical de la Universidad de Chile.

It was the day before Christmas Eve, but the spirit of that time as I knew it was very much absent here. First of all, I was soon to learn that a Christmas tree on a balmy summer day was nonsense, and that Chileans go out to dance instead on such occasions. I had met some of the dancers, who took me to an outdoor swimming pool, where we passed most of the time during the holidays. But one evening was spent at the Uthoffs', where, over dinner and drinks, Lola and I became fast friends. Lola still danced a number of roles in the company's repertory, especially the mother in Jooss's *The Green Table*.

After Christmas, I met the rest of the company and was assigned to learn the role of Don Juan in Uthoff's ballet of the same name. Patricio Bunster, who was soon to join the company Jooss had started again in Essen-Werden, had previously danced the role. He had taken a year's leave of absence to work more closely with The Master. Rudolf Pescht, handicapped by illness, still proved important to me when he, and Uthoff, coached me as the Standard Bearer in *The Green Table*.

There were a few gifted dancers in the company, mostly women, but the severe lack of a sound technique made them all look more like serious students. Of course, I couldn't help showing off some technical bravura during classes, conducted mostly by Lola, until some of the young women approached me, pleading for "real ballet lessons." Knowing that Uthoff strictly forbade his female dancers to follow the classical code of acquiring a technical base for dancing, especially in toe shoes, I rented a studio away from where we worked. There I taught classical ballet to an ever-growing number of dancers from the National Ballet.

It took an incredible amount of time for Uthoff to catch on, until it was impossible for him not to note his dancers' stretched legs and feet; their whole bearing had changed. One of the male dancers, Octavio Cintolesi, had been with the company for several years and sided with me. I held classes from 9:30 to 11:00 P.M., expanding that time after I began to choreograph a pas de deux to music from Stravinsky's *Orfeo* for Virginia Roncal, the most gifted of my students, and myself. Eventually Uthoff, whom I finally invited to look at my work, asked me to consider choreographing the whole ballet, which I did. It turned out to be the first of several.

Taking his cue from this development, Octavio demanded that he, too, be allowed to choreograph a ballet in toe shoes. Uthoff finally gave in and with it came a change in attitude toward classical ballet training that would move the company to greater achievements in the future. In later years, Octavio formed his own classical ballet company in Santiago, and it now counts among the major cultural institutions in the country.

Meanwhile, word had gotten to me about an older lady who had been a dancer in the famed Marinsky Ballet of St. Petersburg, Russia. After following several leads as to her whereabouts, I found her to be living in another part of Santiago, across from the river Mapocho. There she lived with her daughter and son-in-law. Helene Poliakova, Madame, as she later became known, had left Russia with Diaghilev's Ballet Russe. She had graduated from the Imperial Ballet School in 1902 and later danced together with Karsavina and Nijinsky, proof of which she always proudly demonstrated with old photographs. As a teacher, she counted Alice Nikitina and Igor Youskevitch as her most famous pupils. On a train trip in Europe during the Second World War, her husband died in her arms when the train became a target of British bombs. The shock left her in a constant state of shaking, also audible in her voice, a condition she only gradually, and not until after the first years of our acquaintance, was able to shed. She had worked as a ballet mistress in Innsbruck, Austria, before moving to Chile in 1949 at the insistence of her daughter, who had married a Chilean.

Madame turned out to be a wonderful teacher. In her late sixties, with her small head, long neck, white hair, and turned-out legs, she had that unmistakable look of a dancer. I became the first person to establish contact with her. Nothing extraordinary happened when we first met. She spoke some German and was fluent in French. After I had introduced myself, I informed her about my past career, after which I asked if she would be willing to give me private lessons after rehearsals in the evening. She hesitated briefly but, obviously pleased, made it clear to me that she would not accept any financial compensation. When we did start to work together, I made it a point to present her with a bouquet of flowers once a week.

From then on, every evening, except on performance days or when I was on tour with the company, we met at 9:30 P.M. for private lessons. My evening classes to the dancers of the company had to take a back seat, especially since Uthoff's acceptance of classical ballet training had made it possible to use the company's studio for that purpose, and so the need to hide our activity had ceased. However, the time for those classes had to be shifted to 1:00 to 4:00 P.M., the hours usually reserved for the long lunch breaks and siestas.

The clock never determined my lessons with Madame; we took our time, and it was the most productive time in my career as a dancer. I could already turn, jump, and beat, but she taught me how to use those technical skills so as to bring them to the service of my performance instead of executing them simply as acquired skills. In the ballets Uthoff choreographed, there was, of course, never a chance at air-turns, pirouettes, or entrechats.

Uthoff's process of working on a ballet was extremely slow. It was not unusual for a new work to be in gestation for almost a year. He would try this and that for days on end, which always gave me ample opportunity to improvise or simply fool around. I began to devise ways to alter his choreography while he was trying to concentrate and obviously watching my attempts at improvising around his choreography. Here and there, I would insert some turns, adding some beats, and even venturing into the double-tour territory, steps from the classical ballet vocabulary with which he was not familiar, but always making sure that those steps ended in some kind of dramatic context. Uthoff's personal use of a dance vocabulary could be performed by dancers who lacked any real technique and to my eye resembled gymnastics, executed with lots of expression and feeling.

Uthoff balked but slowly began to change. He noticed that my additions didn't really change his choreographic intentions, or so I thought. I do know that he simply didn't want to admit that he had begun to like what I offered him. It took almost a year to convince him that if he hired Madame Poliakova, his future dancers from the school would be much better material for his ballets. Until now, I had been the only person who was allowed to teach ballet at the school for the National Ballet. After Madame had finally been hired as teacher for the company, several other dancers joined me as I continued private lessons with her. She would become an important part of the company, and her work began to change the look of the company.

After Octavio and I had unveiled our ballets in pointe shoes, Uthoff took to using the pointe shoe method in two of his ballets, without having grasped its unique possibilities. He was best at telling stories through the use of simple steps that were devoid of invention and demonstrated a lack of recognizable dance technique. He had missed out on the opportunity to train himself properly as a member of the Jooss group, and as a choreographer he simply wasn't Jooss. His colleagues, Rolf Alexander, Noel de Mosa, and Hans Züllig, among them had all secretly taken ballet lessons while in England, despite Jooss's early stand against such practice. Jooss himself had ultimately included ballet technique at the school in Essen-Werden, recognizing the validity of its results as a training tool.

Patricio Bunster returned from Germany. During his absence, he had married an English dancer, a product of Sigurd Leeder, a well-known teacher in London at the time. Sigurd Leeder's career had taken him from performing together with Jooss in solo concerts in Germany during the early years of modern dance to a position of eminence within the structure of the Ballet Jooss. As a major force in the company, while also one of its performers, he had developed a distinguished vocabulary for the training of dancers. Joan Turner was a strong modern dancer. She proved especially memorable as the Guerilla in *The Green Table*. Her presence onstage was never less than mesmerizing. Patricio Bunster, together with another new recruit, Jean Cebron, shared the role of Death in Jooss's master-piece, *The Green Table*.

The ultimate Death, Max Zomosa, was to enter the school as a student. Max was still studying at the medical school and conse-quently missed many classes. He didn't seem to know if dancing was what he wanted to do. He had an acute awareness of his limita-tions to becoming a professional dancer. Max was stiff, and his body, unable to bend, ended with feet that couldn't or wouldn't stretch an inch. But he was tall, and knowing that male dancers do not grow on trees, Poliakova and I, with valuable assistance from Joan Turner, who had begun to teach modern technique, were able to arouse Max's interest. Besides being a lamb in human form, we dis-covered that he was strong as an ox, which convinced Uthoff that Max should be taught and trained for the role that would eventu-ally make him outstanding as Death.

It must also be mentioned that Max, by South American stan-dards, was unattractive to women. Later, as a member of the com-pany and when on our tours, it was always Max who helped the women in the company by herding their considerable luggage to their hotel rooms. I knew his wife, a nurse who once administered an injection to my posterior after I had contracted a case of gonor-rhea. Both were still young, although they had three children. It seemed to me at times that Max tried to escape a marital situation that had become too much for him. He was a vulnerable person and very much in need of acceptance and reassurance. We eventually became close friends, always respecting each other, sharing rooms on our tours until our arrival in New York in 1964.

For part of the summer, the company toured either the north or the south of Chile, followed by a six-week vacation period. Having some time ago discovered the charms of Valparaiso, Viña del Mar, Renaca, and other places on the Pacific Ocean, I made it a point to spend my vacations there, swimming in the ice-cold waters, lying in the sun, and visiting the casino in Viña del Mar. Periodically, I became entranced by the possibility of winning money without doing any work and often gambled from 6:00 to 9:00 in the evening and from 10:00 P.M. to 3 A.M.

I had no money to lose, so, after much observation, I played exclusively at the baccarat tables, which could be played standing behind the seated players. Moving constantly from table to table allowed me to place my bets on many tables, and only on the ones where either the bank or the public showed a winning streak. In that fashion, during an eight-hour period, I would win enough money to cover my hotel and food expense for the following day. Of course, the system didn't work consistently, but throughout my almost six-week stay, I spent practically nothing of my own money.

The Uthoffs always spent their vacations in Pucon, in a German-run pension on a beautiful lake. At their urging, I joined them for several summers there. A nearby volcano had spewed its ashes all over the area, including the beach and the bottom of the lake. Long excursions on horseback would take us into wild forests, high up, and very close to the crater of the volcano. It was a magical place, like so many in this country, where luminosity and majesty are played against each other in constant succession over a stretch of almost three thousand kilometers.

When the following season started, I learned and later danced one of the major roles in *Juventud* (Youth), a ballet Jooss had choreographed while in Chile and that had never been performed. Uthoff asked my opinion about costumes for the dance, which I ultimately designed directly on the dancers' bodies. The ballet had music by Handel, and to this day I consider it to have been one of Jooss's major works. With a cast of four women and four men, plus two lead couples, the dance merely hinted at a dramatic tension among the couples, but nothing was spelled out. The dancing and the choreographic configurations were at the heart of the ballet. The vocabulary was pure Jooss, without recalling any of his earlier works. A kind of formality suggested that the choreographer had experimented and in the process broadened his view of dance. *Juventud* had definitely broken new ground for Jooss. Unfortunately, Uthoff retired the ballet without any trace of documentation, and a couple of photographs are all that remains of a dance in which I had the honor to participate. I do not know about Jooss's personal feelings about this particular work of his. At a dinner in New York, after the opening of the all-Jooss program by the Joffrey Ballet, attended by his daughter Anna, her husband Herman Markard, Robert Joffrey, Thomas Skelton, Jooss, and myself, I neglected to address the subject and never saw Jooss again.

Besides innumerable performances as the Standard Bearer in *The Green Table* over the following ten years, I danced the Cavalier in *A Ball in Old Vienna* and one of the gentlemen in *Pavanne for a Dead Infanta* on a program which opened with *Big City*. In 1954, Uthoff choreographed *Carmina Burana* for Elena Aranguiz and me, which, together with his *Prodigal Son*, were considered at home and on our South American tours to be his most important work. As Franz in his *Coppelia*, I was never allowed to leave the stage. More to my liking was his work for me as Petrouschka. Although the climax of my solo demanded several drops onto my knees from a hidden ladder behind the scenery, a feat that left me with painful scabs which the next performance would scrape raw again for the duration of the season, I loved the role and the music very much.

CHAPTER 13
Interlude

That same year, the passing of a kidney stone made it necessary for me to undergo a number of tests. A well-known specialist, the father of one of my students and a friend of mine, Martha Orrego, took me into his care. Only later, and after an operation had finally diagnosed the nature of my troubles, was I told that initial tests had suggested renal failure and the belief that I probably would not see the light of day after three more months. The word had gone around very fast and understandably had not reached me, but it had me wondering why everybody was so nice all of a sudden.

Totally free of symptoms, I entered the hospital one morning for a set of tests. A previous test had consisted of the search for a kidney on my left side, which had refused to show up on a number of x-rays. After I had been pumped full of air, which should have floated any hidden organ out of hiding, it was decided that an operation was the ultimate choice. Another six weeks passed during which the air left my body slowly and painfully through the skin.

Thinking back, I can now say the operation itself and the healing process thereafter were child's play in comparison to the tests administered before. The first had dislodged all the remaining stones that would pass the urinary tract during a two-week period. A daily dose of morphine kept most of the pain under control.

I had become close to the family of a friend who had been a lover. Hector Maglio, his sister Victoria, Señora Emma, and Don Manuel had taken me in like a family. Their beautiful old colonial home, then on the calle Carmen 185, was an important place during most of my years in Chile. The home was a gathering place for actors and other friends. Hector was a member of the Teatro Experimental de la Universidad de Chile and we had met when Uthoff's staging of the ballet *La Leyenda de José* (The Legend of Joseph) by Richard Strauss, demanded the presence of merrymaking actors during my long solo in the ballet. I remember the many joyful evenings spent at the family's home and the elaborate meals served in the dining room that accommodated easily a dozen merry diners. Don Manuel was a manufacturer of large cast-iron stoves for many of the city's restaurants, which he created in a small workshop in the backyard of his home. A front room of the house, facing the street, accommodated a store where Victoria (Toya) sold kitchen utensils, but only at certain, and for her, convenient hours during the day. Señora Emma spent most of the days in her very ample kitchen preparing lunch and dinner with the help of a maid. Another important member of the family, Tia Rosa, Don Manuel's sister, served to spread the news about the rest of the members of the large family during the long Sunday lunch hours. Of course, siestas were a must, only to be interrupted by the chiming of bells from the nuns' convent across the street. Eventually, after I had left the country, the house was removed to make room for a street to be built. The memory of it and its inhabitants, all deceased except for my friend Victoria, remains strong and full of love.

When the passing of the kidney stones was complete, I had to be weaned from the painkillers and morphine. The task of drying and changing my perspiring body four or five times during many of the following nights fell to Hector, while I lay utterly exhausted, mostly unaware of my surroundings. Time and my belief that nothing was seriously wrong with me finally gave me back my strength to face the upcoming surgery.

The operation revealed that I had been born with just one double-sized kidney. A defect in the position of that organ since birth had prevented a complete flow of urine, which had made my kidney read as a cloud on x-rays and which ultimately explained the initial misdiagnosis of possible tuberculosis. The operation was a complete success, but I was advised that any strenuous activity in the future would be considered dangerous. Dancing should be out of the question, and any job that would confine me to a chair became the doctor's order. Little did he know about my willpower.

After just a few weeks, with the incision only partially healed, itching to move, I set out to choreograph a dance for my friend Martha Orrego and myself. Since I was a public employee, the company could not let me dance until after several more x-rays confirmed the success of the operation and the completion of the healing process. With all expenses being taken care of by the government, including the ongoing payment of my salary during that year, I found myself in an enviable position. Martha and I ordered costumes made for dances yet to be realized. We rehearsed at Carmen 185 in the large covered courtyard of the house. The dances turned out to be mostly elegant duets, and in some of them Martha wore toe shoes. We thought the dances were sexy in a sophisticated way. As our intention had been to present them in nightclubs, we deliberately steered away from the then-fashionable acrobatic devices used to keep patrons awake. We secretly wondered if we were in the process of introducing a new trend in club dance entertainment, or if we were simply out of tune.

We hired a photographer and sent letters and snapshots directly to clubs in Santiago and Buenos Aires, when, lo and behold, we received an invitation from a club in Miami to appear for an audition when in the area. They obviously must have confused us with an already traveling attraction, but that didn't diminish our joy when we had received the invitation. However, by now Martha's family had gotten wind of the fact that our intentions were serious, as opposed to what had been perceived as innocent play. Martha's family forbade her to continue her adventure. Her father being a very well-known and respected surgeon made her family part of Santiago's aristocracy. It became clear that we had squandered our time and money. Besides, Martha was a married woman, a fact I had never considered an obstacle. My attempt at rescuing my efforts with another student failed after several rehearsals. She proved a strong enough dancer but totally lacked Martha's sex appeal.

There was still much time to kill before I would be allowed to dance with the company again. I attended classes at my own risk and soon was back taking my private lessons with Madame. When I finally could join rehearsals again after almost a year, I once more proposed to choreograph a ballet, never an easy thing to ask Uthoff. Using Handel's *Fireworks* music, I titled the ballet *Divertimento Real*, or *Royal Divertissement*. I had used the strongest dancers in the company and it became a personal triumph for Virginia Roncal and José Uribe, the ballet's soloists. Those dancers had never been seen to possess such an accomplished classical technique, which ultimately led Virginia to join the Ballet de Marquis de Cuevas in Paris during a two-year leave of absence. My next work for the company, titled *Ensueño*, or *Dream*, to Ravel's *Valses Nobles et Sentimentales* turned out to be a flop and my least favorite ballet. I begged Uthoff to retire it at the end of that current season, which he did, and for which I was grateful.

While I was working on *Divertimento Real*, Pauline Koner, who had been a major force with the José Limón Dance Company, arrived from New York to set her *Concertino*, a work for three woman, on the company. Pauline was a brilliant dancer who also had excelled in solo concerts of her own works. John Taras came next to stage his *Design for Strings*. Here was a man whose association with George Balanchine and the New York City Ballet produced great excitement among all of us. His classes proved especially interesting to us because of their emphasis on speed. Eventually three of Birgit Cullberg's ballets entered the repertory, and there was finally some challenging classical choreography to be danced. Birgit Cullberg, a Swedish dancer and choreographer, was working as a choreographer for the Royal Swedish Ballet and had studied with Kurt Jooss and Sigurd Leeder. Her ballets *Miss Julie*, *Medea*, and *Lady from the Sea* presented another welcome challenge to the company. Also, the roster of dancers was soon to be enriched by the addition of Hans Züllig, Rolf Alexander, Noel de Mosa, and Sigurd Leeder, as the head of the school. Hans Züllig, although already at an advanced age for a dancer, still possessed remarkable skills in addition to a glowing presence whenever he stepped on the stage. His performances in Jooss's *Big City* and *The Green Table* are unforgettable. The same must be said about Noel de Mosa who, in addition to her brilliance as a dancer, had feet that must have been the envy of every classical ballerina of that time. Rolf Alexander, Noel's husband, was a good but messy dancer. He was tall and best as Death in *The Green Table*.

Sigurd Leeder's classes faintly resembled the classes at the Folkwang School, but his were more demanding. His classes for us teachers caught my attention most. His teachings about relationships on stage among dancers and their surroundings in general included fascinating examples that became a staple in my later teaching. The communication between two dancers, as in a pas de deux, for example, raised issues about eye contact at various distances. Of course, the dynamics, onstage dimensions, the diagonals, the vertical and

horizontal possibilities on any stage were also included in his theo-
ries. But the emphasis remained upon the many facets of communication in space. We practiced in silence, back-to-back, facing upstage,
facing downstage, eyes never meeting—in short, every possible combination. After a while, it felt as if we were acting with our bodies,
speaking with our bodies without uttering a word, only divining the
meaning of small involuntary gestures that crept up on us.

Those became revealing possibilities for me, just like the seemingly simple exercises involving the stretching of individual fingers
to ensure a firm projection of an accusing finger, or the gentle touch
on someone's head or shoulder. Hands became the soul of a dancer
for me. If a dancer's body can speak volumes, the hands reveal generosity of spirit or the opposite. The same holds true in the use of
feet. The best dancers know how not to punish the floor they are
dancing on. The feet should become the closest accomplices of the
floor when dancing, and their mutual caresses produce the loud-
est bravos. Unfortunately, the majority of classical dancers galumph
about, the sound of their feet competing with the music. Most of
the women do not know that there is something between the tips of
their toes and the heel that asks to be used. Toe dancing is painful
to watch when I become aware of the toe shoe as a torture instrument on the dancer's feet. Much of what I love and what I hate
about the execution of classical dancing, or dancing period, comes
ultimately from my belief that there is only good or bad dancing.
Obviously, the result of good dancing has as its roots the sensibility
of good, creative teachers, as opposed to a teacher whose knowledge
is limited to stringing together a number of classroom steps.

During the second half of the 1950s the company embarked on
several tours that brought it notably to the cities of Montevideo
in Uruguay and Buenos Aires in neighboring Argentina. After our
arrival in Buenos Aires and subsequent bus ride to the ferry that

would shuttle us to Montevideo, Rolf Alexander, who was scheduled to dance the role he had originated as the *Prodigal Son*, became
the victim of a severe back injury. Without my knowledge, Uthoff,
Lola, Rolf, and Noel had already conspired as to who would ask if
I would be willing to learn the role while in Montevideo. Lola was
finally chosen to break the news to me. Of course, I felt flattered
but feared that the role required much more time than the few days
allowed before its performance. In the end, we all agreed to cancel *Prodigal Son* in Montevideo to have time for me to be groomed
adequately for our season at the prestigious Teatro Colón in Buenos
Aires the following week.

Rolf rehearsed with me every morning after class, when the rest
of the company performed that same evening. I used every spare
moment to retrace the steps I had learned that morning, in the process trying not to imitate Rolf's interpretation of the role.

In the end, the premiere in Buenos Aires received enthusiastic
approval from audiences and critics alike, and with Rolf's assurance
that I had danced the role as if it had been mine since its inception.

During our engagement at the Teatro Colón, the José Limón
Dance Company was performing at the Teatre dell Opera in the
same neighborhood. The Chilean Ballet had become the toast of
the town after the presentation of the Jooss program, with which
the company had introduced itself. On one of their free days, a
few of the Limón dancers came to see our performance, obviously
intrigued by Jooss's fame in the dance world. Tom Skelton, who was
the Limón Company's stage manager and lighting designer at the
time, came backstage after the performance to check and admire
the light plot for *The Green Table*. After this, my first encounter
with Tom, who eventually would become my companion for thirty
years until his untimely death, we headed for a nearby joint for beer
and discussion about ballet versus modern dance, with both aesthet-

ics still very much at war with each other. Classical ballet, with its established and codified vocabulary over more than three hundred years, saw itself challenged with what would eventually be termed "modern dance," personified at the turn of the twentieth century by the American dancer Isadora Duncan. Since then, much has been accomplished under the banner of modern dance, which consists of a variety of dance styles as opposed to the classic academic *dance d'école*. I would meet Tom again in 1964 in New York when I danced with the Chilean Ballet as a guest.

I had not seen my family for ten years and finally asked for a three-month leave of absence. I left Santiago in the beginning of December 1960, landing at the airport in Düsseldorf, just half an hour from my hometown. The flight, still by propeller-driven plane and lavish by today's standards, had made stops in Buenos Aires, Rio de Janeiro, Halifax, Dakar, and Madrid before landing in Düsseldorf. It was quite possible to gain a pound or two on those trips. On arrival at the customs area, I spotted Mother, Father, and Else. They were desperately trying to identify their son and brother, but to no avail. Not until I stepped directly in front of them did they recognize me.

Having lived in a different country among people who had become my adopted family, and having grown into an adult man, I sensed that our *wiedersehen* produced some consternation at first. Nonetheless, Mother's tears seemed unstoppable and Father dropped his cigar while trying to embrace me. For my part, having happily adjusted to a Latino lifestyle, with embraces and kisses on the cheeks an everyday norm, I found myself having to adjust to a much less outgoing lifestyle once more. And adjust I did. We spent a warm, comforting Christmas and New Year's Eve together. Germany was at the height of its economic miracle *Wirtschaftswunder* years, during which everything seemed to be possible and available. Father's business was booming again; he drove a beautiful green Mercedes

Benz, and the house, like many others in the neighborhood, sported a completely new façade. New wallpaper graced all the rooms, and a large bathroom with tub and shower had been added. Other beautifying renovations had been made outside. Gone were the shed and the old outhouse, and in its place there were flagstones, bushes, and trees. The laundry room had been remodeled into my parents' bedroom, while the wall that had separated their old bedroom from the living room had been removed to accommodate a dining area.

My parents had obviously tried hard to impress me, and I thanked them for their heartfelt intentions. What they did not and could not perceive was the fact that in my mind I was coming home, not expecting anything more than what I had left behind all those years ago. Memory had played a trick on me. I had remembered the forests with their huge trees, but those trees did not seem huge anymore. In reality, nothing had changed. It was I who had changed, and I had to blame that sense of betrayal on myself. The family did their best to make my stay comfortable and nice. The obvious strain between my two sisters caused the only negative and at times unpleasant moments during my visit. Mother took me to uncles, aunts, cousins, nephews, and others faintly related to the family. Several newspapers sent their interviewers to the house. For my part, I accepted the attention because it made my parents proud.

Twice I was able to escape to visit old friends in Hamburg and Wiesbaden in addition to Trude Pohl at the Folkwang School and at her home for a pleasant dinner. Kurt A. Jung had made a career as a radio announcer and commentator in Hamburg. A former dance colleague from Göttingen had switched from dancing to acting and directing. We spent some precious time together over dinners, theater, and late-night drinks and conversations.

In Wupperthal, I visited with Erich Walter. Erich had taken some ballet classes from me in Nüremberg, when I had been dancing the pas de deux from *Les Sylphides* as a guest with my friend Jutta. He now had become a well-known director-choreographer in the pre–Pina Bausch Wupperthal. I also attended one of his productions and got reacquainted with my partner from Berlin, Denise Laumer, who had joined his company.

My best time was to be had in Wiesbaden. Two of my friends who had studied with me at the Folkwang School lived here. Denise had become a ballet dancer at the local Opera House. Karl Heinz and I had lived together in Essen-Werden. We had had the kind of youthful infatuation where we would have killed for each other. He had become a poet and had changed his name to the more poetic-sounding Christian. The two had remained close friends, and we spent most afternoons and late evenings at the many gay clubs and bars frequented by members of the occupying American Army. Those smoke-filled places were not like the bars that served to find a partner for the night; they were rather more like meeting places for like-minded individuals who came to eat, meet friends, drink, and listen to records. Flirt, yes, but not in an aggressive way, more like evoking jealousy in whoever happened to be your date. Dancing and laughter pervaded those places in a city where in the summer an important modern music festival took place. Hans Werner and I attended one of the festivals together, where music could be heard at every possible venue, day and night.

March 3 had marked Mother's birthday, and soon afterwards I left, to spend a week in Paris. I arrived on a late afternoon. From my hotel, in the vicinity of the Eiffel Tower, I proceeded to walk through the city until the following morning. Exhausted and with large blisters on both feet, I finally stopped at a brasserie for an early breakfast. For the rest of the week, I hardly took the time to sleep. On that first morning, I searched for and found the then-famous Studio Walker where I would take my daily ballet lessons from the famous Madame Nora. I also moved to a hotel on the rue Lécluse, just a short walk from the studio. The morning classes began with the arrival of the pianist, an elderly lady who beat the keys as if cleaning them for the real pianist. As soon as she would sit down, she began to play, and it became clear to me that the exercise on the barre was a fixed affair.

On that first day, I followed and learned the sequence of exercises which invariably began by stretching with one leg on the barre to the front, side, and back, to be repeated in *à la seconde* and *arabesque* positions. At the age of thirty-three, that wasn't my idea of a day's beginning, but I survived, hoping it would be habit-forming. Madame would only make her appearance just before the dreaded *rond de jambe en l'air*. If you had taken it easy until now, you'd better get it right when she arrived—and not just to get your money's worth. Madame had a way with sarcastic remarks, followed by a vicious laugh that never failed to remind me of Margaret Hamilton in *The Wizard of Oz*. That said, I must admit that she was an excellent teacher, and our relationship remained always cordial. The following year when I came to Paris for an extended time, it was Madame, Nora Kiss, who was responsible for my dancing as a guest of the companies with which she had contact. We often lunched together in the studio's little cafeteria, but our very professional relationship ended one day when I took a class from another teacher. On that point, Madame was unforgiving.

During this, my first week in Paris, I would spend the rest of each day strolling through the city, visiting the Louvre and the Rodin museum, picturesque Montmartre, and the Place Pigalle at night.

It was the end of March, and the air was still cool when I boarded the plane back to Chile. Left to worry how I would be able to smuggle a tape recorder, a heavy and cumbersome item at the time, a camera, half a dozen tights, and assorted gifts into Chile, I spent considerable time in the plane's WC before my arrival in Santiago. I emerged finally dressed with six pairs of tights beneath my slacks, two heavy woolen sweaters, and my Rolleiflex camera on my back under my new camelhair coat. It still being late summer in Chile, I had to endure more than an hour's worth of extreme discomfort, but refused to shed my coat. To my great amazement, the customs officer simply waved me through when my turn came. I didn't know that my waiting friends had taken care of the situation beforehand.

A few days after my return, I announced to Uthoff that I wished to leave at the end of the 1961 season. However, I did agree to return after having spent a year dancing and receiving further training with different teachers in France.

While in Chile, I choreographed the dances for Ravel's opera *L'Enfant et les Sortilèges* and intensified my private lessons with Madame Poliakova, who had been the person who urged me to go and seek work with a classical company. The 1961 season brought us again to Montevideo, La Plata, and Buenos Aires, before the usual performances in Santiago, which led me closer to departing time once again.

CHAPTER 14
Paris

In the beginning of 1962, I found myself again in Paris at the same hotel and just a few blocks from the famous Studio Walker. Paris hadn't lost its magic, and I hope it never will. The Marquis de Cuevas had died, leaving Raymundo de la Rain, his Chilean nephew, in charge of Le Grand Ballet's directorship. Raymundo had been a friend in Chile, where his family was well known among the country's aristocracy. His interest had been in the design of rather extravagant scenery and costumes for ballet. The National Ballet's repertory had obviously no use for his work, and Raymundo's taste in dance definitely did not coincide with the local company's aesthetic.

At one point, I had mentioned to him that Paris would be the place where his work would catch attention, without knowing at the time that the Marquis de Cuevas, the founder of the Grand Ballet de Marquis de Cuevas, was a relative of his. My arrival in Paris coincided with Raymundo's production of *Cinderella* at the Théâtre des Champs-Elysée in which Geraldine Chaplin made a minor appearance. Chaplin, at one point in the ballet, was carried onstage and lowered in the center, after which she executed a series of pseudo-oriental movements and steps (in soft slippers) and was then carried out again, to thunderous applause. Raymundo had installed me backstage in the wings to watch the performance. We enjoyed a pleasant dinner after the show, reminiscing over our times in Chile. I do not remember the names of the dancers who danced the title roles in the production, as it was Geraldine Chaplin who had been the attraction. I missed the production of the *Sleeping Beauty* with Rudolf Nureyev, who had shortly before caused a stir in the dance world because of his defection at Le Bourget airport from the visiting Kirov Ballet.

I was now taking two classes daily and, in order not to run out of money, accepted an invitation to dance a featured role in the ballet scene of Gounod's opera *Faust* in Rouen. I had become friends with several dancers who also took classes at the Studio Walker and who lived in similar hotel accommodations on the rue Lécluse. We banded together and often cooked our meal on a small hot plate, which, of course, was strictly forbidden. Mostly I lived on a daily baguette, a piece of Gruyere cheese, and a quart of milk.

Jean Michel Damase, the French composer who had written the score for the ballet *La Croqueuse de diamants* by Roland Petit, was a friend. I had met him when he was in Chile with one of several European companies who visited on a fairly regular basis. Jean Michel lived with his mother on Boulevard Malesherb, but on his free weekends they would spend time at their charming old country home, not far from Auvers Sur Oise where van Gogh and his brother Theo are laid to rest. The small house in which van Gogh had occupied a room, the room that he painted and which has become one of many of his signature paintings, stands right next to a country graveyard with two very small stones, inscribed simply "Vincent" and "Theo." On several occasions, I was a guest at the country house and never missed the opportunity to visit the graveyard. The place seemed magical in its simplicity, with large groups of blackbirds taking to the skies almost constantly.

Jean Michel would often take me out for dinner when he happened to be in Paris. We had entertained a short affair and remained best friends afterward. Because of his status as a well-known composer, he was always invited to social and theatrical events in the city, and he would often take me with him. On a number of occasions, we attended performances of chamber ensembles at the private residences of titled members of Paris aristocracy, always followed by a sumptuous buffet-style dinner. Memorable among those outings was a performance at the Casino de Paris, followed by a lavish party given in honor of the one-thousandth performance of a then very famous French star. One number in the show that especially captured my attention took place when an enormous cigar box opened slowly, revealing twelve practically naked and very tall beautiful black women. They left the box one by one and just walked in the most seductive way to the strains of well-known melodies of the time. One by one, they placed themselves back into the cigar box, which slowly closed as the curtain fell. I loved the combination of humor and sex appeal, the two opposing idiosyncratic expressions formulated into one.

The large foyer had been decorated and furbished very elegantly after intermission. When leaving the auditorium, we were ushered to our numbered table. A large buffet and lots of champagne made sure that everyone had fun. Dancing followed dinner, and, to everyone's amusement, Rudolf Nureyev and the French rock star Johnny Halliday were seen dancing together on top of a table.

Ballet in Paris was at a very low point. At the Opéra Comique, the female dancers sported hairstyles fashioned after Brigitte Bardot, the French movie star. A male dancer in toe shoes was a sensation. The Paris Opéra Ballet, although it counted a number of wonderful dancers, didn't have anything of substance to dance, and Maurice Béjart, who had just evolved as the new voice on the horizon, was uniformly denounced as a faker by the ballet establishment. I am personally not and never have been a fan of Béjart, but at the time he gave audiences relief from the generally mediocre offerings in the City of Light. Roland Petit, whose work I admired, was preparing, it was rumored, a show that would launch his wife Zizi Jeanmaire as a singer and dancer in a revue called *Zizi*. In the mid-1960s, *Zizi* opened on Broadway with Tom Skelton's lighting.

Another very different balletic spectacle with Ludmilla Tcherina as its star, libretto and sets by Jean Cocteau, and music by Antonio Vivaldi, became a sensation. Together with Janine Charrat's ballet *Abraxas*, those two spectacles dominated the dance scene for a while.

But the high point during my entire stay in Paris was the unforgettable pairings of Eric Bruhn with Sonia Arova and Rudolf Nureyev with Rosella Hightower in a performance of excerpts from the famous ballet classics. With sublime understatement, they shed a totally new light on those familiar steps.

At one point Pierre Lacotte, the artistic director of the newly formed *Le Ballet JMF*, short for *Jeunesses Musicales de France*, approached me. Pierre had been one of the stars at the Paris Opéra Ballet and was in the process of hiring dancers for his small government-sponsored touring ensemble. During our conversation, I told him about my background as a dancer, teacher, and choreographer, and mentioned that I soon had to return to Chile for another season before being able to come back to Paris.

Soon after I had arrived back in Santiago, I received and signed a contract for the 1963–64 season as dancer and ballet master for Lacotte's company. While back in Chile, I choreographed the dances for a musical comedy: *Madame Amneris, Vidente* (vidente means clairvoyant), with music by Francisco Flores del Campo. The musical starred Silvia Pinero, a well-known and beloved Chilean comedian. Afterwards, I made it known to Uthoff that I was leaving Chile for good at the end of the National Ballet's season. I loved Chile and hated the idea of leaving so many friends behind, many who had become family to me.

Something in Chile seemed to have changed during my long absence. A small group of dancers had become politically active. How active I would never know, but they had begun using slogans that reminded me of my own country when slogans were used to inflame people's minds. As a consequence, my departure proved finally less traumatic, given those circumstances.

This time I traveled the less expensive way, by boat from Buenos Aires to Genoa and from there by train to Paris. The relatively small ship carried mostly Italians, and the voyage turned out to be a living nightmare. My assigned cabin was shared by a young priest who, after having realized that he was to spend a whole week in close quarters with a ballet dancer, proceeded to lecture me at every encounter about the sins of the flesh. Three times daily, at mealtimes, we all took our places at a large communal table, facing the same faces that spoke only Italian. The never-changing antipasto dishes were followed by a main course that also varied seldom. Around the pool, babies and children outnumbered adults by something like 4 to 1. The deafening noise kept me below deck for most of the day, while the evenings provided two choices: watching an Italian film while children would be crying and babies vomiting, or listening to the lecture by my cabinmate. Insufficient lighting during evening hours made reading impossible, so I enjoyed my nightly peace on deck, watching the stars reflecting in the moving water.

From a few passengers my age I found out that most people on board were being sent back to their homeland after supposedly having failed to make a decent living as immigration-hopefuls. Europe, especially Germany, was still in short supply of laborers, and that was exactly where the younger generation was headed. Eventually, a few of them were able to change places with their countrymen at the table, which gave us the opportunity to converse in Spanish, which those few young Italians had learned very well.

When we docked in Naples for several hours, I enjoyed a wonderful lunch at a seafood restaurant before returning to the ship. It would still be the rest of the day and another night before the boat would drop anchor in Genoa. We disembarked during the morning hours, after which I made my way to the train station, where I purchased a ticket to Paris for a sleeping car bunk bed. The train was to leave at night, which gave me plenty of time to stroll through the city. At boarding time, I found that I was to share the sleeping compartment with three women and four other men. In spite of my watchful eye all night about the possible crossings from bunk to bunk, the trip proved uneventful in this regard, and I finally succumbed to sleep.

Back at my hotel in the rue Lécluse, I phoned Lacotte to announce my arrival and to get instructions about upcoming rehearsals. Soon I would meet my fellow dancers, eleven in all, including Lacotte and our *régisseur*, Don Spottswood. Don was an American who had danced with the de Cuevas company and served as its *régisseur* before joining our little group. Record players were still the norm at rehearsals, with studio space being rented at various locations.

Dessin pour le six by John Taras (variously named also *Designs for Strings*, or *Design for Six*) was the first ballet entrusted to me as ballet master for the company. I had learned the ballet from Taras himself when he was in Chile, and I had danced it numerous times. Eventually, I would dance the ballet again at the Théâtre des Champs-Elysée with Ghislaine Thesmar and on our extensive tours throughout

France, on the island of Corsica, and in Tunis. During my tenure with the company I choreographed three ballets: *Triangle*, with music by Parish Alvars; *Le Songe d'une nuit d'été*, a free adaptation of Shakespeare's *A Midsummer Night's Dream*, with text by Mario Bois and music by Mendelssohn; and *Preface*, to music by Miles Davis. *Preface* had its premiere at the Salle Pleyel in 1964. *Le Songe d'une nuit d'été* was presented on a program with Pierre Lacotte's ballet *Hamlet*, on the occasion of the four-hundredth anniversary of Shakespeare's birthday in 1964, with the Château de Saumur as backdrop.

One of our troupe's major events was its participation at the Festival in Aix-en-Provence with *Les Noces*, choreographed by George Skibine, with costumes and décor by Nathalie Gontcharova. The ballet received many performances after our four-week engagement in Aix-en-Provence. I personally scored a major success with the role of the father, a role Skibine had extended into a major characterization as the ballet progressed.

The season ended with performances in Tunis. Tunis will always play an important part in my memory because it was here that we received the news of President Kennedy's assassination. All activity ceased on that day, and we cancelled the performance. Some members of the company expressed their frustrations, suggesting that the killing of presidents was possible only in America. Kennedy was the most respected and loved American president known to my generation of Europeans. We all loved his image and for a very long time grieved after his very untimely departure from the peaceful world he had created, not just for us, but for his America as well.

Our engagement took place in an amphitheater on a private estate that bordered on the ocean. Our individual dressing rooms, which also served as our sleeping quarters, were located below the auditorium of the amphitheater. However, the area's mosquito population made it impossible to get any rest during the night, which proved to be the only setback during an otherwise very successful, week-long engagement. Breakfast, lunch, and dinner were served in the main house, just a short walking distance from the theater.

Back in Paris, I choreographed two ballets for the newly formed Paris Festival Ballet under the direction of Ramon Solè: *Un Jour…* with music by Mozart, and *Printemps,* which I had choreographed for the Chilean National Ballet to music by Jean Michel Damase.

To my surprise, Uthoff and Lola came to Paris. His motive was an offer for me to appear with the Chileans at the newly constructed New York State Theater in New York City. I was to dance my original role as the Youth in his *Carmina Burana* on opening night. He hoped this ballet would propel him into the ranks of important choreographers. On the second program, I was to dance the title role in *Prodigal Son,* the role I had taken over from Rolf Alexander, who had retired from dancing when still in Chile. He later left Chile and divorced Noel de Mosa to marry a rich Chilean woman who helped him form a baroque music ensemble in Germany. I had also hoped to dance the Standard Bearer in *The Green Table,* but it turned out that such a possibility had created major controversy among some members of the company, who felt that as a guest with the company I should not dance two major roles during this important visit. But the opportunity to dance in America caused me to accept the contractual obligation to step also into minor roles should injuries make it necessary.

After I completed my contract with the French company, I departed for Santiago to attend rehearsals and dance a number of performances before the beginning of the tour that brought us again to Lima, Peru, before heading to New York, Montreal, Philadelphia, Chicago, Pittsburgh, and a number of other cities in the United States.

When I left Paris, I had contemplated remaining in the United States after my contractual obligation with the Chileans. My friend

Jutta Brintz was living in California with her American husband and her two children. Jutta had maintained contact during the many years since our departure from Konstanz am Bodensee in Germany in the hope that one day I would join her in establishing a ballet school in Bakersfield, where she lived. Jutta would ultimately confess to me that Bakersfield was a godforsaken place if ever there was one, and that she approved of my decision to remain in New York.

CHAPTER 15
America

I roomed with Max Zomosa, who had been my roommate since he became a member of the Chilean company. On entering our hotel room, we spotted a television set in one corner, and for the longest time Max sat and watched in awe. He had never seen a TV set before, since acceptable transmission had not yet come to the Chilean Andes. It was Thanksgiving in the United States, and after a long stroll on Broadway with Lola and Max, we dined on turkey (all we could eat) in a delicatessen between our hotel and Union Square.

Rehearsals were to begin the following morning in one of the studios in the State Theater. After breakfast at the hotel's corner coffee shop, where I discovered cheesecake, in which I indulged at every opportunity, Max and I crossed the street to the studio where, to my surprise, I ran into Tom Skelton. It was news to me that Tom had been engaged as lighting designer for our New York repertory. Since our fleeting acquaintance in Buenos Aires, we had had no contact with each other. During subsequent rehearsals, our professional relationship developed into a gradual attraction.

The company's wardrobe, which included all of our rehearsal clothes, had not arrived, and so this, our first day of rehearsal, had to be conducted in street clothes. We did our best to move through the choreography, taking care to be in the right places so Tom could sketch a preliminary light plot for our two programs. Tom seemed to be in need of a constant supply of coffee by his side. He had brought Edward Burbridge with him, a friend and set designer. They would eventually collaborate on several Broadway shows and sometime in the 1970s Ed would create a beautiful backdrop for one of my ballets. The following day our costumes arrived, and we were finally able to dance each ballet to Tom's satisfaction.

The company received a warm reception in New York and, as was to be expected, *The Green Table* was singled out among all the other works. The opening program on November 10, 1964, included *Carmina Burana* by Uthoff and *Calaucan*, with choreography by Patricio Bunster, in which I appeared in a small role as one of the Conquistadors. On November 12, the second program was introduced with *Prodigal Son*, followed by *Alotria*, also by Uthoff, in which I danced with Maria Elena Aranguiz as the Equilibrists. *Alotria*, an untranslatable title that means something like "gone fishing," and *Calaucan*, which was based on a poem by Pablo Neruda, were short ballets, with the latter being the better of the two. Having read about but never having seen Balanchine's *Prodigal Son*, I had thought it a mistake to bring Uthoff's version to New York. Although rooted in the Jooss tradition, Uthoff's treatment of the ballet's subject lacked Jooss's mastery of communication through simplicity of gesture and movement through his unique choreographic voice. Comparison to Balanchine was, of course, inevitable in the dance world of New York, and the same fate would be accorded to *Carmina Burana*, which was known in New York in John Butler's famous version. But *The Green Table* carried the day. The weeklong performances were all well attended, especially by the Hispanic population in the city.

One event of major importance was my reunion with Ella Haacke. She had been my student in Chile. Her parents were Germans who had come to Chile via Bolivia, where Ella was born. Ella's father strongly opposed her wishes to take ballet lessons but relented after he discovered that I was German. Eventually, we became close friends. In 1952, Ella moved to New York to attend college, where she met and married Earl Bailley. They had three sons, and lived happily in Westbury, Long Island.

Ella and Earl made their way backstage after the first performance in New York, and it would soon be made clear to me that my future had been decided upon. It didn't take long for them to convince me that Bakersfield, California, was the wrong place for me to be and that after my return later from Puerto Rico, the company's last performance venue, I was to move with them to Long Island. Over dinner after the second show, we began making plans for my future in America.

Their first concern was the acquisition of a green card for me, on which Earl would get to work immediately. My visa was good for three months, and in my favor was the fact that the quota for German immigrants was open. Ella and Earl would be vouching to support me, should I become a burden to my adopted country. I told them that I had pledged to stop dancing after my obligation to the Chileans and that I wished to dedicate myself to teaching and perhaps to choreography, should the opportunity arise. Old injuries on my right foot had by now made it necessary to exercise for an hour before being able to take class. After getting out of bed in the morning, I limped around for a while before I could walk normally.

Earl had decided that with my looks and a beautiful girl as a partner, I would make a fortune in America. Of course, his suggestion included the use of skimpy costumes in a nightclub. After all, Earl was the quintessential all-American male. He had a heart of gold, and both of them were totally accepting of my sexuality and later of Tom. We spent several delightful days at Christmas time together with their young sons, Roger, Douglas, and Bruce. Earl did succeed in making me the proud possessor of a green card in a very short time. The agent in charge of my interview at the downtown immigration office in New York seemed to have just one question for me, after having verified my occupation as a dancer: "I hope you are the kind who dances with their shoes on." My affirmative answer sealed my future.

How long I lived with Ella and Earl I do not remember. I had already spent many days and nights with Tom in his loft on Second Avenue on top of La MaMa, Ellen Stuart's theatrical creation which had begun to be influential in the New York theater world, before finally moving in for good.

Ella had introduced me to the owner of a ballet studio at Carnegie Hall, where she would take a class whenever she was in town. For my part, I had decided that perhaps by taking lessons I would eventually make contact with people in the field of dance. One day, as I entered the elevator of the Carnegie Hall building, I found myself to be the only passenger besides a lady I immediately recognized as Alexandra Danilova. I managed a timid nod in her direction, which she acknowledged with a smile. It turned out that she was teaching the class I had planned on attending at the studio of Fedor Lensky.

Shortly after the class started, Madame appeared at my side to inquire about where I came from and with whom I had studied. She knew Helene Poliakova, and told me that I moved like Eric Bruhn. Bruhn had been my idol, and if I ever had dreamed to dance like anyone, it would have been him. We chatted away while I was trying also to concentrate on the exercise. In her charming, strong Russian accent, she confided to me how difficult it was to teach amateurs, but that she had to make a living. Her class consisted mostly of women with very little knowledge and physical aptitude for classical ballet, and my heart went out to her.

She must have been and obviously still was an extraordinary coach to many young and not-so-young professional dancers. Whenever she finished demonstrating a combination during floor work, the whole class would clamor for a repeat because of their inability to retain the sequence of steps only professionals are able to master. As it was difficult for Madame to demonstrate the combination exactly in the same fashion as before, which she found unnecessary anyway, she would very clearly pronounce the words "just do." She soon realized that every combination sank instantly in with me, after which she advised the class to watch Heinz. From that moment on, my place during class was in front with her, and the clamoring for a repeat demonstration ceased.

I obviously was extremely flattered to be of service to Madame. After several days, she reminded me how difficult it was to succeed in New York and suggested that I join her friend, Nathalie Krassovska, who headed a ballet company in Dallas, Texas, where I could act as teacher and choreographer. Of course, I declined the offer in order to stay in New York with Tom. She also asked me to teach her class on occasions, so she could accept some guest appearances out of town. Thus began my teaching career in America. Her guest appearances became more and more frequent after she felt assured that the students loved and approved of my teaching. Not long afterwards, she followed Balanchine's invitation to join the teaching staff at the School of American Ballet in New York.

In 1965, I auditioned for the American Dance Festival to be held at the State Theater. Curiosity had driven me to experience what it would be like to dance in an American modern ballet. I was accepted and danced in Doris Humphrey's *Passacaglia*, in which I was also to understudy the male lead, plus Sophie Maslow's *The Village I Knew*. This served to remind me of how far and different modern dance in America had been from its European counterpart, especially in Germany.

For many years after the Second World War, Germany seemed to have been in denial about its modern dance past. I personally had

had the feeling that everywhere in German theaters the trend was to follow safely the example of America, where modern dance still struggled for acceptance, but where the Balanchine aesthetic had become the rule. Many voices of modern dance had been silenced during the Hitler years, and even Wigman's contributions seemed to have vanished from audiences' minds after the war. With the gradual disappearance of the solo concert dancer, modern dance as I still knew it lost much of its original power in Germany. Even the other "great ones," Kreutzberg and Dore Hoyer, did not leave behind them anything else but the memory of themselves and, therefore, had no influence in the future development of modern dance in their country. The arrival of Pina Bausch in Wupperthal signaled a new and very different view of what dance is able to con-vey. Her influence has spread over continents, but her contribu-tions will not, at least in my mind, determine the role of modern dance in the future.

The pianist who accompanied my classes at the Carnegie Hall Studio had taken ill, and in his place Mr. Lensky had sent me a gentleman who had the astounding ability to play the piano with only two fingers, the way I write on my computer. After about five minutes, with students rolling their eyes and my nerves on edge, I asked him to please stop playing and proceeded to teach the class with thumb and middle finger snapping the tempo. The offended pianist left and reappeared with the owner, Mr. Lensky himself, who in an admonishing tone told me that my behavior would be unacceptable in America and that I was to continue to teach with "HIM." I finished the class and promptly resigned.

Some of my adult students—among them Jane Herman, who much later served as general manager for the American Ballet The-ater, and Ann Waugh, a dancer with a distinguished career as an educator in the history of dance, who later founded the Dance

Library of Israel—visited with Thalia Mara at the National Academy of Ballet. They informed her about my availability as a teacher. Thalia Mara had been a student of Anna Pavlova and had founded the prestigious National Academy of Ballet. That same evening, I received a phone call from Thalia Mara asking me to teach a class at her school the following morning. A well-organized institution, the National Academy proved a very pleasant place to teach, with an assigned accompanist who turned out to be one of the best I would ever encounter. The school offered graded classes in ballet every morning, with academic classes proceeding throughout the afternoons. Ms. Mara had also written several books about the teaching of ballet. Her school was one of the best of its kind in New York.

Classes for adults could be accommodated only on Saturdays, so Jane and Ann, with a number of other students from my class at Carnegie Hall, rented space and hired a pianist. Mondays through Fridays, we met at a small studio on the corner of Eighth Avenue and Fifty-third Street, above a fish store. Here my classes, with Jane and Ann's encouragement, eventually developed into rehearsals for several dances we later presented around town, in churches and museums.

Tom had taken it upon himself to organize reviews and articles about my work in South America and France. Eventually, we sent them to various companies and to a few soloists in the United States and Canada. The first response came in the form of a phone call from Celia Franca, the founder and director of the National Ballet of Canada. Celia invited me to come to Toronto for an interview and to discuss the possibility of working with her company as a choreographer. I had been scheduled to receive my green card in a few more days, and several days after that important event I was on my way to Canada. It turned out to be a very happy first meeting. Celia had been especially intrigued by the fact that I had danced in Jooss's major ballets. She herself had danced with the Jooss group when she was a dancer in England. I stayed as a guest in Celia's home with her conductor-husband Jay and her many cats. As I was a cat-lover myself, we spent inordinate time comparing cat stories. After the day's work at the studio, she would cook and prepare different meals for each of them, while also finding time to feed Jay and me.

At the studios of her National Ballet, I got a good look at many of her excellent dancers, among them Martine van Hamel, Lois Smith, Veronika Tennant, and Earl Kraus. In Joanne Nisbet and her husband David Scott, ballet mistress and assistant ballet master, I found friends whose encouragement was of great help to me during my work with the company. I dined several evenings at their home, in the company of James, their beloved dog. In the span of several years, I choreographed three works for the National Ballet of Canada: *Adagio Cantabile*, to music by Tomaso Albinoni, *Rondo Giocoso*, to music by Gioacchino Rossini, and *Celebrations*, to music by Gabriel Fauré. In all, my association with everyone at the National Ballet of Canada remains in my mind as one of those pleasant experiences I will cherish forever. Celia to this day has remained my loyal, wonderful friend.

All the work I did for the National Ballet of Canada was done during the National Academy's vacation, but several events would soon happen in rapid succession. Tom had been approached by Barbara Weisberger, founder and artistic director of the Pennsylvania Ballet, to design the costumes, set, and lighting for a production of *The Sleeping Beauty*. Barbara had gotten a major grant from the Ford Foundation, and her company was in the process of turning into a professional ensemble, after years of being stuck with the minor-sounding image of "civic ballet."

Tom was having lunch with Barbara at a Manhattan restaurant. We had plans after lunch, which caused him to ask me to come to the restaurant at a certain hour, at which he thought that Barbara would have long been gone. As fate would have it, they had just ordered dessert when I arrived at our appointed time. After introductions, Barbara and Tom continued their conversation around the production Tom seemed to have agreed to design. By my estimation, they must have had a wonderful time together. So by now, Barbara would casually finish her sentences by asking me, "Don't you think so?" It did not take me very long to figure out if they were talking about the scenery or a scene in the ballet. After one more "Don't you think so" I began to volunteer my opinion on how I would approach the ballet if I had the fortune to have my own company. Of course, that statement demanded further comment, and so I rattled on about the many possibilities that existed in presenting the story of the sleeping princess.

Why compete with the Royal or Kirov Ballet that had the proper resources and talent to present such large-scale ballets? Why was it not possible to take a totally different route, streamlining its production values and having the score arranged so that the pantomime could be kept to a minimum or be completely deleted to make room for uninterrupted dancing? The possibilities for change could be endless if the right people were willing to take such chances. I do not remember what other opinions I voiced, but it seemed to have made enough of an impact for Barbara to ask me to come to Philadelphia to discuss those possibilities further.

While teaching during the National Academy's summer session, I had received several invitations from teachers who had traveled to New York with their students to come and teach in their respective cities for a short period of time. I dreaded to leave New York, and yet, as much as most teachers hated such work, it augmented our income, something not to let pass so easily. My first reaction was to call on Bob Joffrey. Bob had been at our New Year's Eve party at the loft, and we had had dinner several times after performances when Tom's work with the Joffrey Company at City Center had ended. My question to him was what to charge. Next

I consulted a map of the United States to find out which of the places offered to me to teach for one week was closest to New York City. It turned out to be Akron, Ohio. A short phone call to Nan Klinger, who was one of the teachers who had traveled the previous summer to New York with a number of her students, confirmed my teaching schedule for one week in September 1966.

Summer session at the National Academy over, I flew to Toronto to stage *Adagio Cantabile* for the Canadians. I remember the pleasure I had working with the dancers there. Their willingness to experiment with different movement and their respect and readiness to learn made for a joyful collaboration.

Back in New York, I took the train to Philadelphia, where I met the dancers and staff of the Pennsylvania Ballet. I watched a class given by Barbara and made a mental note of some of the most interesting dancers in the company. After class, Barbara, Ballet Master Robert Rodham, and I joined for lunch, where I was offered the job of staging and choreographing *The Sleeping Beauty*. I believe we agreed to begin work in approximately two weeks to give me time to sort out how to approach the work to Barbara's satisfaction. I remember Barbara telling me that her board wanted a "name," and that Violette Verdy from the New York City Ballet had agreed to dance the lead. I had met Violette when living in Paris, and, knowing her sunny disposition, I was looking forward to working with her.

My teaching job at the National Academy kept me at the school until 1:00 P.M., after which I had to hurry by taxi to the train station to make the 1:30 P.M. to Philadelphia. Rehearsals began at 4:00 P.M., ending with a mad dash to reach my train back home at 11:30 P.M. The ride back to New York was used to take stock of that day's work and to make notes for possible changes and additions in the choreography. I always used the daily three-hour trip to Philadelphia to prepare for the work to be done that same day.

Left Heinz in Paris, 1963.

Below Tom Skelton in New York, mid-1960s.

Heinz in Akron, early 1970s.

Ohio Ballet, Heinz's *Adagio for Two Dancers*, 1973. Photograph by Ott Gangl.

Christopher Stygar and Kim Abkemeier, Heinz's *Summer Night*, 1974.
Photograph by Ott Gangl.

Heinz with ballerina Carol Thwaite, rehearsal for Heinz's *Schubert Waltzes*, 1975. Photograph by Ott Gangl.

Above Ohio Ballet in rehearsal with Paul Taylor for his *Aureole*, undated. Photograph by Ott Gangl.

Left Ohio Ballet in Cleveland, 1982. Photograph by Ott Gangl.

Upper Right Tom Skelton working on lighting design for Ohio Ballet, undated. Photograph © Martha Swope.

Lower Right Heinz, Laura Dean, and dancers in rehearsal of *Patterns of Change*, undated. Photograph by Ott Gangl.

Upper Left Farm in Stockton, New Jersey, purchased by Heinz and Tom in 1969.

Lower Left Tom on patio of New Jersey farmhouse, undated.

Upper Right Heinz with favorite cat, James, undated.

Lower Right Tom in Piazza San Marco, Venice, 1989.

Above Heinz with his mother and nieces, early 1980s.

Left Heinz, a rare smile, late 1980s. Photograph by Ott Gangl.

Left Heinz, late 1980s.
Photograph by Ott Gangl.

Below Heinz and Tom on their
second visit to Italy, 1992.

Heinz, circa 1992. Photograph by Ott Gangl.

Barbara had surprised me with the news that Henry Danton, formerly with England's Royal Ballet, had previously been engaged to stage a number of variations and the Rose Adagio after Marius Petipa. Petipa's choreography for *The Sleeping Beauty*, with music by Tchaikovsky, dates back to 1890 and is now considered one of the greatest achievements in ballet history. As I had been placed in charge of staging my own version of the production and choreographing the ballet, it became clear to me that the inclusion of Petipa's choreography would undermine my whole concept of the ballet as I had envisioned it when I had signed the contract. Obviously, there was nothing I could do but try to make the best of it. Barbara explained to me that she wished to retain the original feel of the ballet, while at the same time creating a different version that would meet with the technical and financial limitations of her company.

Next I was informed that Melissa Hayden would replace an injured Violette Verdy. Melissa, also of New York City Ballet fame, was to join the company one week prior to opening night on November 26, 1965. During the three months leading to the premiere, I had worked with a very fine young dancer, Carole Luppescu, on the role of Aurora, together with the young Alexei Yudenich as Prince Charming. Rose Marie Wright, a very tall and gifted fifteen-year-old, was my choice for Carabosse, a role that ended up being danced on opening night by Sara Leland, also a noted dancer of the New York City Ballet. Leland's name was obviously a box office draw, while Rose Marie Wright was an unknown entity unable to attract paying customers, an inevitable fact in the world of entertainment. Anne Byrne, a beautiful young woman who later married the now famous Dustin Hoffman, had danced with the New York City Ballet before joining the Pennsylvanians. She was pregnant at the time but agreed to mime the role of the Queen. As I eventually changed the mime to a dancing role instead, Anne wisely withdrew, and Barbara herself became the Queen. We worked daily at a feverish pace, and every minute was taken up with changes, corrections, costume fittings, and arguments—in short, all the things that go into the preparation of a ballet everywhere.

I had some misgivings about Melissa's arrival only a week before our opening. There were a number of transitions in my choreography she had to become familiar with. I had been told that she had danced the role of Aurora only recently in Germany. But Melissa was unaware that a different version of the ballet awaited her, which was the source of my misgivings. However, I also knew that a seasoned dancer like Melissa Hayden would have no problem adjusting to the changes made during any choreographic process. I had changed many mime sequences into dance phrases before she finally arrived. The company was very relaxed, well rehearsed, and confident. Carol Luppescu had learned all of Aurora's variations, including the additional choreography. With Melissa, Barbara, and General Manager David Kanter in the audience at the Academy of Music, the company danced the whole ballet so Melissa would have an idea of what this version promised and looked like.

The run-through over, Melissa took to the stage to confront the conductor Maurice Kaplan as to the correct tempo for her first solo. No matter what the conductor did, none of the tempos pleased Melissa. Tensions grew, and the company became visibly intimidated by the verbal assault from ballerina to conductor. I could already see the carefully constructed production, built on a small kingdom with its central character, a sixteen-year-old innocent princess, falling apart at the seams. At one point, it became necessary for me to stop the proceedings in order to assure the company that they were doing a beautiful job. I then terminated the rehearsal for the day, expecting that a night of reflection and rest would recharge everyone's energies toward a positive collaboration.

During the following days, rehearsals were divided between the teaching of new and additional choreography to Melissa, to which she responded favorably, and which later in the day progressed to the Rose Adagio and the Grand Pas de Deux. Those rehearsals with Alexei Yudenich were especially heartbreaking because of the star's insistence that he repeat the same lift over and over again. She obviously didn't approve of him as her partner. Alexei ultimately suffered an injury to his back, but his determination won out. After a few days of rest, he was back and ready to lift again.

On Thanksgiving Day, after Melissa and I had shared a late supper, the sky began to clear and for the first time a sense of working in unison became a possibility. Still, the work had many stylistic problems. My personal contributions had dominated the production, but were at odds with Petipa's Fairy variations, his beautiful Rose Adagio and Grand Pas de Deux. Petipa's sublime choreographic inventions called for a production on a scale that a company with the resources of the Pennsylvania Ballet could not afford. To make things worse, in the last act, later to be performed separately under the title of *Aurora's Wedding*, I was responsible for the choreography for the four Oriental princesses, while Puss in Boots, the Blue Bird Pas de Deux, and Red Riding Hood and the Wolf had also been staged after Petipa by Henry Danton. It became obvious that the mixture would have serious artistic ramifications, and it would definitely not be I who would benefit from it. Sure enough, the glowing notices in the Philadelphia papers were soon to be harshly contradicted in the *New York Times*. When the company revived the ballet the following year, the Philadelphia press also trashed the production.

Tom Skelton's designs in brown and sepia colors, with Aurora and the Prince in pristine white, had the look of an old engraving. Aurora's tutu, topped with pink petals and soft pink sleeves, was a stunning contrast to her surroundings. The sleeves were meant to camouflage any kind of angularity of the arms of the wearer. To our distress and before her entrance, Melissa had ripped the sleeves from the bodice of her costume, which greatly marred the effect of her entrance and turned Tom's admiration for the dancer into disgust for her unprofessional conduct.

Barbara Weisberger, who had diligently rehearsed the Polonaise which marked the entrance of King and Queen, ravishingly took to the stage. She also acted as mother, confidante, and psychiatrist to keep things flowing as smoothly as possible with the interaction of so many talented people. The company had been augmented to fifty dancers for the production, with several dancers from E. Virginia Williams's Boston Ballet and a couple of men, besides Melissa Hayden and Sara Leland, from the New York City Ballet.

CHAPTER 16

Back in New York

Our loft on Second Avenue had its advantage where space was concerned. It also provided ample room for friends to spend the night. Jennifer Tipton, still Tom's right hand before embarking on her own successful career as a lighting designer, along with Tom and myself would sometimes leave the theater, where both had been working until late, to attend a midnight showing of the latest James Bond movie. It was not unusual to arrive back at the loft at 2:30 A.M. to broil some steaks. After washing the dishes, I invariably would find them both deep asleep, usually on the floor with an empty beer can beside them. We always made sure that Jennifer was comfortable with a blanket and a pillow before we would withdraw to our bedroom. By morning, Jennifer would be gone, to reappear again around noon, when both would continue their work on the current show.

As the two daily classes I taught at the National Academy always took place in the mornings, I was free from 1:00 P.M. until my evening lessons on top of the fish store on Eighth Avenue. During my free time, I often dragged our laundry to the laundromat or did some cleaning chores at the loft. One of the disadvantages of the loft was the fact that exactly beneath our bedroom window, on street level, a Chinese laundry and dry cleaning establishment sent its exhaust fumes into our open bedroom window during the sum-

mer months. The fumes once almost killed our friend Edward Burbridge while he was having a nap on a hot afternoon. Tom found
him just in time and took him to a hospital, where he spent several
hours before being released.

The loft was large, messy, and very dark. Lighting consisted of
a number of light bulbs, camouflaged in black-painted coffee cans
hanging from an equally black ceiling. There was definitely no sign
of a lighting designer living there, but the exposed brick walls, black
ceilings, and overall studied shabbiness were very much in vogue in
1960s New York. Whenever any one of us entered, it was necessary
to move around with utmost caution so as not to collide with chairs
and tables until our eyes had adjusted to the darkness around us,
even though we had left the lights on. During the day, enough light
filtered through a large window facing Second Avenue. Every couple of months, we swept the floor from one end to the other, adding
yet another coat of paint, usually black or gray, to give the illusion of
a perfectly clean living space. It also gave us the opportunity to collect books and paperwork from the floor into neat stacks on tables
Tom used to work on. Our bathroom, the best-lit and most desirable
place in the loft, had a huge old-fashioned cast-iron bathtub. Tom
and I, like most of our friends, were smokers. I collected many hundreds of different cigarette-box wrappings, glued them to the walls
of the bathroom, and covered them with a shiny waterproof finish.

To get to the loft, one had to ascend two staircases. In many
instances, after dark, it was possible to detect the presence of figures
under the lower part of the staircase, mostly obviously fornicating
couples. Only once did we have to report a stabbing. The door to the
building was always open and unprotected unless La MaMa's small
auditorium was awaiting its clientele for a performance. The door to
our loft had two large locks and a complicated system for bolting the
door from the inside. The rent was only ninety-five dollars.

On one of the coldest days of that winter in 1965–66, we decided to search for a somewhat smaller living space in the Village, a space that would be more manageable. With Tom on his way to a successful career on Broadway and with my teaching, we found we could afford something in a slightly higher scale of rent. An agency on Christopher Street sent us to an apartment, still occupied, at 29 West Tenth Street, ground floor with a backyard garden, for $135.

When a young woman opened the door, I spotted a honey-colored cat sitting at the other end of the approximately twelve-foot-long entrance hall, which prompted me to inquire if the animal came with the apartment. Mrs. Schwarz turned out to be delighted at my interest in her cat since Mr. Schwarz was highly allergic to the animal. The apartment had a bathroom with a shower stall, a small bedroom, a charming combination kitchen-living room, which led to a glass-enclosed porch, which in turn led to a garden. It didn't take us more than ten minutes to make up our minds, realizing the apartment's possibilities. After racing back to the agency, stating our intention, and making a date to sign the papers, we returned to inform Mrs. Schwarz that we wished to pick up the cat the following day. It would still be a matter of at least three weeks before the Schwarzes would have to move out. Another two weeks would be needed to paint, replace the floor covering to our taste, and build a partition around the kitchen area that would serve as a table on one side and as a bar on the other. During that time our cat, whom we named James, would be living with us in the loft so we could get mutually acquainted. Tom had never been fond of cats, having grown up with just a dog. James would soon change his mind.

We took enormous pleasure in working on our apartment. There were many things to be accomplished before everything met with our approval and until we felt satisfied with the results of our labor. Leaving the loft proved no easy task. Our personal possessions were minimal, but to rid ourselves of all the accumulated junk, as Tom had lived a number of years in the loft before I had moved in with him, was a major and ultimately expensive affair. Yet after completing a satisfying move, there is always a feeling of starting life anew, and that's exactly what we did. James became the center of our lives, and, practically broke, we began to spend much more time at home, learning to cook for pleasure and for friends, and at the same time being totally absorbed by our respective occupations.

Tom's work on Broadway coincided with the Joffrey Ballet's first season at the City Center Theater. The Joffrey Ballet, with Tom's lighting, opened a new window through which dance would be seen. The two elements, dance and light, became practically inseparable and remained like that for many years. I firmly believe that Tom's lighting on Broadway during the last half of the sixties was partially responsible for that category's inclusion in the Antoinette Perry Awards in the 1969–70 Broadway season. That year, Tom received his first Tony nomination for the musical *Indians*, with a book by the playwright Arthur Kopit and music by Richard Peaslee.

While on leave in New York when he was in the army, Tom had attended his first dance performance, given by the Martha Graham Dance Company. As he would always recall, there was a woman in front of the theater who turned out to be Isadora Bennett, at the time Graham's manager. Isadora, who eventually became a close friend when she was the general manager of the Joffrey Ballet, took him by the hand, urging him to attend the performance free of charge, an opportunity at the time for soldiers on leave. His description of that performance always centered on Jean Rosenthal's lighting, which would ultimately determine his future career.

Tom's early years as lighting designer included work for the José Limón Dance Company, for which he also served as stage manager, before being assigned by Sol Hurok to light the Inbal Company of Israel. His career in dance lighting continued with Paul Taylor,

Pearl Lang, Ballet Folklórico de México, Foo Hsing and the Air-irang Korean Ballet Troupe, before his longtime involvement with the Robert Joffrey company. While lighting an off-Broadway play by Arthur Kopit, he came in contact with Jerome Robbins, who was directing the play. Robbins invited Tom to create the lighting for his *Dances at a Gathering* at the New York City Ballet. Tom's lighting designs also graced some of Agnes de Mille's and Antony Tudor's works. Among the famous faces he lit on Broadway were Sandy Duncan, Rex Harrison, Katharine Hepburn, Dustin Hoffman, Lena Horne, Jason Robards, Rudolf Nureyev, and Maureen Stapleton. Norman Roston's play *Come Slowly Eden*, about the life of the poet Emily Dickinson, with Kim Hunter, who had starred in the film *A Streetcar Named Desire* as Stella, was both directed and designed by Tom at the Lucille Lortel Theatre downtown.

In 1966, while the Academy of Ballet was on a short vacation, I made good on the promise to teach for one week in Akron, Ohio. The classes were held in a small basement of a private home that had been converted into a narrow studio space with a ballet barre, the device used by dancers to hold onto when exercising during the first part of a class. I concentrated exclusively on barre work and its correct execution, as the hard and slippery floor made any attempt at work away from the barre impossible. That week seemed interminable, and although I was grateful to Nan Klinger, who had engaged me, for her hospitality and the students' desire to please, I yearned for the day of my return to New York.

It was a few months later that Nan Klinger, in conjunction with a physical education teacher from Kent State University, Gay Nokes, arranged for a master class to be held at the campus of the University of Akron. Prior to the master class, I had been asked to act as one of the adjudicators for promising young choreographers from the Kent State University School of Dance and others from around the state, which also included a gifted group from the Ohio

State University in Columbus. Following the event, I was to teach a master class for the students of the Kent State University School of Dance, followed by a second class the next morning, before moving on to Akron for the general master class.

The gymnasium at the University of Akron, like any other gymnasium with a highly polished floor on top of concrete, was also not a desirable place for a ballet class. I was still a relative newcomer to the United States and had taught only in New York. But this was the other America, the small-town America in need of education, where thousands of young people's dreams of becoming dancers created a need for qualified teachers. About eighty students, selected by their teachers from various communities, but mostly from studios in nearby Cleveland, attended the class. It soon became obvious to me that the majority of them would never be able to set foot on a legitimate stage as dancers. Too many of them lacked the physical attributes for a career in classical dancing. But most of them seemed not to be aware of their shortcomings, which made their determination to become ballerinas a sad spectacle to me. But there was some talent, too, and a small number of them would later succeed at dancing on a professional level.

As at all master classes, there were onlookers, and when the class had finished, one of them introduced herself to me as Catherine Firestone. It turned out that Kate had been a soloist with the renowned Sadler's Wells Ballet, later to become the Royal Ballet of England, dancing under her maiden name, Catherine Boulton. At dinner that evening, the seed was planted for a Summer Dance Institute, which Kate and I founded in the summer of 1967. All the schools in the area were informed of the event, and we asked the teachers to bring just the most talented of their students for auditions. From those auditions, we were able to recruit four different graded classes with no more than fifteen students per class.

My teaching schedule in New York continued while Kate, with Gay Nokes, worked on the University of Akron to secure the necessary studio space for our four-week venture planned for the following summer. Back in New York, I attended practically every show on Broadway, including the New York City, Graham, Taylor, and Joffrey companies. Tom's influence had made it possible to obtain free tickets to all the shows. Attending opening night parties of the plays or musicals Tom had worked on was always a special treat for me.

Out of curiosity, I attended an audition for the musical *Hello, Dolly!* which had opened recently and which I had seen from the first row mezzanine. I counted myself among what must have been hundreds of aspirants and ended up among the five finalists. Everything had gone well, the waltzing and the rest of the dancing, until the tap dancing routine was announced. I immediately explained to the dance captain about my inability to tap dance and asked to be excused. But the captain wouldn't have any of it and urged me to do anything that came into my mind while crossing the stage when my number was called.

I did, doing cabrioles and double tours, after which the captain told me that Gower Champion wished to have a word with me. Approaching the apron of the stage, I faced the man I had so often admired on the screen. He held out his hand and told me that as an accomplished ballet dancer my bearing would perhaps interfere with the style of ensemble dancing the show required. Of course, I was flattered and my head must have visibly swelled to have been spoken to by the great man himself. From the way they looked at me, everyone in the wings seemed to think that I got a starring role. I decided to remain aloof and left the theater as soon as I had dressed.

It now was time to return to Canada to choreograph my second ballet for the National Ballet. *Adagio Cantabile*, my first ballet for the Canadians, had proved successful, and now it was *Rondo Gio-*

coso, to music by Gioacchino Rossini, a gentle spoof of the romantic period in ballet, that had aroused my curiosity. After the premiere, Celia and I discussed the possibility of yet another work for her touring company the following year. *Rondo Giocoso* was also successful with audiences and dancers on its tour through the Canadian provinces. At the same time, I received an offer to teach at the National Ballet School in Toronto from its director, Betty Oliphant, which coincided with an offer from Barbara Weisberger to act as assistant ballet master for the Pennsylvania Ballet. As both offers would require me to move away from New York and my life with Tom, I declined and continued teaching in the city.

CHAPTER 17

The Dance Institute of
the University of Akron

As time drew near for our summer course at the University of Akron in 1967, I planned for my four-week absence from home. Tom's schedule had become frantic and unpredictable with sudden departures to the opera house in Brussels, where he was lighting operas and Maurice Béjart's ballets, and where he eventually directed and lit the opera *Carmen*. Now our cat James became a problem. We sometimes had left him with enough food and water when we went on short weekend trips to Fire Island. However, on recent trips to the island we had taken him with us. In the end, I took him with me to Akron, which turned into a major problem, as I was unable to find an appropriate place to stay with him. Gay Nokes, who was in charge of organizing space for classes, seemed somehow to be at a loss when it came to finding a place for a gentleman from New York with a cat. Eventually, I found an apartment, not far from campus, into which I had to smuggle James.

The teaching load proved gruesome, with Kate teaching pointe classes to advanced young women, as well as mime, the art of tying ribbons on shoes, and in general about neatness in class. I taught ballet technique on all four levels, besides character and modern dance in the Jooss tradition.

After the first week of classes, Kate invited the wife of the then-president of the University of Akron, Mrs. Norman P. Auburn, to watch one of my classes. According to Kate, Mrs. Auburn was a widely traveled and sophisticated woman with excellent taste in the arts but with little patience for amateur presentations. We supplied her with a comfortable chair and a large supply of coffee, which we hoped would keep her from falling asleep. When she arrived, she proved to be a very charming and gracious woman with a gravelly voice who showed enormous interest in the class and who, after the first hour and a half, asked if it would be okay to stay. And stay she did, for the next three classes. And so, Kate and Kay, as we called them, talked me into an agreement that would bring me to Akron every second weekend after the completion of the summer course. Kay had no background in dance or any of the other arts, but during her frequent travels around the globe she had attended many theater, opera, and dance performances, which ultimately had shaped her awareness of excellence in the arts.

I made friends during those four weeks. First of all, there were the students, most of them innocently devoted and committed to a life in dance, who helped me make up my mind about the continuation of what I had termed the Dance Institute, eventually to be under the administration of the College of Fine and Applied Arts. There were the parents of one of my students, Gena Carroll and her husband Bill, a pathologist, who invited me to their home for dinner and who later let me share in their family life. Bill was born in Moscow and Gena came from Odessa. They had met in Germany, where Gena had studied dentistry, before they immigrated to the United States. We became friends when I returned to Akron from New York, where I was still teaching. Gena had made it clear that I was to stay in her home, which would save the Dance Institute the expense of having to put me up in a hotel. She also put herself in charge of collecting tuition, to be delivered to a special account at the university, and to act as chauffeur and as the general liaisón with the teachers of the institute's students. Her home also often served as a meeting place between the teachers and myself.

Sometimes I gave special lessons to the teachers, because I found it important that they understand what and what not to do with the students who had been selected to attend classes at the institute. From what I had seen at various recitals given by some of them, it was obvious to me that much damage was being done by asking very young students to execute steps in toe shoes that would be challenging even to young professionals. A number of their students were still children whose bone structure was still incomplete. The teachers themselves had no professional experience as dancers and taught mostly by watching professionals in action or by taking an occasional class when on visits in New York. Few ballet teachers who command schools in the many small towns know enough about the negative consequences of bad training. And it is not always those teachers who are at fault, but parents' demands to see their daughters on the tips of their toes in pink tulle dresses. On the positive side, there also were schools run by retired professionals from the several companies with Russian names who had toured the country, but mostly in major cities. However, I believe that at the time my approach of working directly with the teachers proved fruitful for all of them.

My weekend engagements involved teaching four classes daily, on Fridays, Saturdays, and Sundays. After the daily teaching load, I eventually decided to work with eight of my most advanced students on the process of making a dance. I used two of my best young women as soloists in pointe shoes, while the other six formed a chorus in soft slippers. In order not to compromise the students' technical capabilities, I kept the steps simple, focusing instead on interpretation. The ballet turned out to be about women who are left alone in time of war. As a springboard, I tried to convey images of the German sculptor and graphic artist Käthe Kollwitz.

As time went by, I continued to add technical challenges to the ballet I eventually called *Elegiac Song*. It proved the longest-surviving work in the repertory of Ohio Ballet, the company I later cofounded with Tom in 1968. After partial completion of the dance, Kate had asked me to show it to an assembly of university teachers and staff, including President Norman P. Auburn and, of course, his wife Kay. That event culminated in a meeting during which Kay asked me to prepare a full program to be given some time in the fall of 1968.

By now I knew it was time to seek counseling about this whole Akron venture from someone I trusted. Tom came to Akron, watched a rehearsal of *Elegiac Song*, then watched me teaching, and fell in love with the concept of creating a chamber ballet. His involvement and encouragement were responsible for the formation of what was to be called the Chamber Ballet, resident ballet at the University of Akron. The company was renamed in 1974 as the Ohio Chamber Ballet for incorporation purposes. At the company's first appearance at New York's Delacort Theater in 1976, its name was changed once more, to Ohio Ballet, after several requests from the company's presenter.

At first, Tom had made it his task to interpret my concept to Kay Auburn and many others at the university, whose vision of ballet went as far as girls in tutus on the tips of their toes. My English vocabulary was very inadequate at that time, since I had never used the language before my arrival in the United States. Tom was perfectly able to translate my poor vocabulary, which saved a lot of time and misunderstandings. In other words, his involvement was essential on all levels, including fund raising and communication with the Women's Board of the University of Akron, the organization responsible for supporting our first concert. Without his contributions, artistic and administrative, there would never have been an Ohio Ballet.

I finally produced a program of three ballets: *Micro Concerto*, *Elegiac Song*, and *Rossiniana*. The dances were tailored to the students' capabilities. We hired a friend of ours, Evelyn Rassias, who had created the costumes from Tom's designs for the Pennsylvania Ballet production of *The Sleeping Beauty*. We worked together with absolute professional integrity, to the dismay of some of the university's personnel, but also to the delight of others who praised our standards. We won the unflagging support of Kay and Norman Auburn.

CHAPTER 18

The Chamber Ballet: Resident Ballet
of the University of Akron

October 12, 1968, marked the Chamber Ballet's first performance. It was an exciting event, especially during the days leading up to the first performance. Tom had trained a small crew as our electrician, stage manager, and wardrobe mistress: Bill Smith, Betty Loui, Peggy Smith, Tim Snyder, Christine Crumrine, and the late Sharon Hollinger joined the crowd. This dedicated group spent years together, and our relationship matured into lasting friendships.

After our first season at the intimate, nearly four-hundred-seat Kolbe Hall on the campus of the university, we planned the seasons to come. It was agreed that the following January, the middle of March, and May would be the times of our annual seasons, as well as the already established October, or fall season. By necessity, I had to choreograph a new work for each of those dates. Rehearsals began at 8:00 P.M., after the last class of the day, and lasted until late into the night during my two monthly visits. The following year, it became obvious that my presence would be required on a weekly basis, which made it necessary to drive the 420 miles from Stockton, New Jersey, where we now lived, to Akron, Ohio, and back, every weekend.

The seasons at Kolbe Hall coincided with the widespread use of marijuana and other substances on campuses around the country. For several of my ballets at this time, I used rock music, a device that proved successful to lure a new and young audience to dance performances. The addition of a dance to classical music, and at times the combination of both, made such programming perfectly acceptable to the students. In fact, the 7:00 P.M. performance was soon expanded into additional 10:00 P.M. and midnight shows in the theater, filled to the brim with students, many dressed in hippie attire and some seemingly under the influence of drugs.

CHAPTER 19

Summer Festival (1969)

Free outdoor performances, in front of an audience unaccustomed to the art of dance, had been an enormous pleasure for me as a performer with the Chilean National Ballet. As a result, I found it to be my duty as the cofounder and artistic director of the Chamber Ballet to introduce the uninitiated into a world they had not known to exist, and at the same time to take the fear out of the word "ballet." Thus, armed with years of experience in dealing with the ups and downs of performing under the stars, I trained my young dancers, while Tom prepared his staff for our first outdoor venture. I had received a warning from the dean of the College of Fine and Applied Arts that too many dangers would be lurking in downtown Akron to expose our young dancers in revealing outfits during the hours of darkness, and that the hour of lunchtime would be more appropriate for our adventure. However, I knew what a beautifully illuminated performance at night could do to an audience. During my entire career, I have never underestimated or played down to audiences in small towns, and after our first performance I had proven my point. My company was not to be confused with some lunchtime entertainers trying to elicit a condescending smile from a handful of office workers munching their sandwiches.

The father of one of my students, proprietor of a lumberyard, provided us, free of charge, with enough material to construct a primitive but firm platform on top of an ice-skating rink on Akron's Main Street. Three male dancers, with Tom and the rest of our staff, worked all day long and into the night to build the stage. A semicircle of steps halfway around the rink made for ample seating on five ascending levels and with plenty of room for folding chairs above the top level of stairs. Our first weekend performance was reported by Cleveland's TV channel 5 with the statement that "a miracle happened in downtown Akron." Our audiences grew from performance to performance, from year to year, and eventually thousands of families came to the many parks in Akron, its surrounding communities, and to Cleveland and other venues throughout northeast Ohio. The portable stage became in time a sixty-by-thirty-two-foot solid structure, equipped with sophisticated lighting towers, a twelve-foot-high black back wall, and an increasingly improved sound system. The company's music director since 1973, David Fisher, always accompanied a number of ballets in our repertory with live piano music. David's association with the company began during the search for a pianist when the company had gotten permission for a production of Robert Joffrey's *Pas des Déesses*. Several of my ballets to piano music, especially *Schubert Waltzes*, *Scenes from Childhood*, and *Songs without Words*, were later to be created in cooperation with his exceptional gifts as a pianist.

One of the high points of our thirty years presenting the Summer Festival happened during a ten-year stint in the city of Warren, sponsored by that city's Second National Bank. The bank spent over twenty thousand dollars to advertise our first performance weekend. Attendance at those Friday and Saturday evenings would at times reach proportions typical for a famous rock group, and not once did we play down with mostly popular works. As a matter of fact, Balanchine's *Concerto Barocco* made the entire audience rise to its feet from its lawn chairs and blankets at the ballet's conclusion and got hundreds of unemployed steel workers using the words "Balanchine" and "pointe shoes" as if they were lifelong ballet fans.

Other communities where it was always a pleasure to perform included Hudson, Medina, Lorain, and Aurora. For thirty years, Ohio Ballet reached out to Akron in its many parks and surrounding communities. After my retirement in 1999, in the summers of 2000 and 2001, three parks in Akron were the only remnants of a once vibrant activity, which provided dancers and staff with valuable workweeks and audiences with many weeks of free pleasure.

It must be noted that dancers had not been paid until the company turned professional in 1974. After that date, it was up to the board of trustees to raise the money to present those summer performances for free. They did so consistently over the years, understanding very well their importance to the community. It was only during the late seventies that the city council began to sponsor part of this important outreach program for its citizens. About this time, the concept would come to the attention of other communities, and the bookings began to fill the entire summer.

CHAPTER 20

Stockton, New Jersey

In August 1969, Tom and I purchased a farm in New Jersey with a twenty-year mortgage. The rent on 29 West Tenth in New York had risen considerably over the past four years, and we figured it would soon match the mortgage payments for a beautiful property in a part of bucolic New Jersey, where the Delaware River acts as the border to Bucks County, Pennsylvania. The decision to buy the farm turned out to be the best deal anyone could have made, and at just the right time. However, after having to purchase two cars, in addition to the down payment for the property, we again found ourselves momentarily broke. I had to give up my teaching job at the National Academy in New York as a result of my now increased involvement with the company in Akron. Tom's work on Broadway had just earned him his first Tony nomination for *Indians*, and with it a certain security within that kind of free-lance profession.

That same year, in order to keep a number of my student dancers who would graduate from high school the following year with our fledgling company, I planned a dance program in the Theater Arts Department of the University of Akron that would let its students graduate with a Bachelor of Fine Arts degree. For some of them, we raised money for tuition, books, and sometimes food. As members of the Chamber Ballet, they were qualified to receive credits and permission to plan classes around our rehearsal schedule. During the company's lay-off periods, the students were allowed to make up for classes lost when on tours. From then on, I was an employee of the University of Akron with the title of director/choreographer.

Valerie Grieg, a retired dancer from the Australian Ballet residing in the United States, joined me eventually as a teacher, once classes for the university program had begun. By the time our first eight students had graduated from high school, Valerie and I had auditioned and accepted several more applicants for the college program, most of them from out of state. They sooner or later became the first solid base for what was still the Chamber Ballet. I myself, not having grown up in a high school or college atmosphere, became more and more disillusioned with the red tape and waste of time under college rules that make it impossible to train a young person for a professional career as a ballet dancer. This is especially true when it comes to young women who need close to ten years to master the art of dancing professionally in toe shoes. To make the training of a future ballet dancer at all possible, I had made it a point to admit only those students who already had a previous and solid background as a student of ballet. After only a short time, I refused to attend any of the faculty meetings, at which the major topic had previously been the size of a new coffeepot.

At this point, I also must admit that at any moment, and even after years of Ohio Ballet's existence, I would have left for good if my efforts to create something special had been seriously interfered with. Yes, I had Tom to defend my actions, but what ultimately would always prove us right regarding our common endeavor, namely to be above the ordinary, was the moment when the curtain would be lifted to reveal the results of our work. By the time our first crop of dancers finally graduated from the university, Valerie Grieg had left, and I had lost a valuable teacher. She, too, was a professional, unable to cope with academic rules and their waste of time. None of my teacher colleagues from New York was interested in coming to Akron, Ohio. All of them had predicted that any effort of such dimensions as ours, in a place like Akron, would fail dismally, a belief that ultimately only nurtured my stubborn determination to prevail. I had to hire teachers who turned out to be incapable of producing dancers of a professional caliber.

By now the relationship with our friends the Carrolls had suffered a severe setback. Gena, whom we had named the company's executive secretary during the formative years, would eventually join Tom as an associate director, a decision we had made as compensation for her generosity as our host and her work for the Dance Institute. Arrangements of such a kind had their counterparts in other cities where companies like ours had began to sprout. And so our decision to rent our own place became a major issue which would make our independence seem like a betrayal of sorts to the Carrolls. Gena was a woman of an extremely dominant nature, which made her unable to forgive anyone who challenged her authority.

When the company was incorporated as the Ohio Chamber Ballet, it turned professional. It was Tom who established a board of trustees. Dancers now needed to be paid, even if only a little, but the money had to be raised.

As a student company, we had performed in a few high school auditoriums in cities not far from Akron. Norman Israel became our first general manager. A tall, corpulent man, he had worked for a number of artistic organizations, and through his contacts we made our first excursions into theaters outside Ohio. The tours would eventually attract students for the college program, as our relationship with the university was explained in our printed programs. Unfortunately, this also caused us to be perceived by our audiences as a student company, albeit an excellent one.

Finding adequate space for making new dances had been solved by assigning us a small building that had been a Baptist church before having been acquired by the university. Within its walls were staged Robert Joffrey's *Pas des Déesses*, Gerald Arpino's *Reflections*, Anna Sokolow's *Rooms*, and Ruthanna Boris's *Cakewalk*, in addition to many of my own works, among them *Adagio for Two Dancers*, *Summer Night*, and *Schubert Waltzes*.

The Civic Theater in downtown Akron, one of the Moorish palaces with stars and moving clouds in a simulated sky, had become our post-Kolbe Hall performance venue. With the EJ Thomas Performing Arts Hall under construction, to be opened in 1973, I prepared for the move into the new theater with a full evening production of the story of the Ramayana. The choice of Bali as its site came after I had listened to a number of records of Balinese gamelan music. I so admired its celestial sounds that for a long time it was the only music I listened to. The sound could be heard constantly when I was spending time at the farm, while at the same time I read practically everything available about the island and the colorful characters of a story that had captured my interest. Ultimately, I chose Balinese gamelan music for the first and third act, while the second act was danced to Colin McPhee's gamelan-influenced *Tabu Tabuhan*.

Saastras turned out to be the most sumptuous production the company would ever attempt and for which I had to augment the number of participants to almost fifty. Members of the company danced all the major roles, with minor ones distributed among advanced students of the Dance Institute. A large number of very young students, hidden behind and under elaborate masks and costumes, served as an army of monsters in a fight with monkeys, culminating in a battle between the hero Rama and the monster Rawana and leading to the marriage ceremony of Rama and Sita and the finale of the ballet.

Tom had engaged A. Christina Giannini, who created a stunning array of costumes and masks and from then on became the
company's permanent costume designer. Tom's wonderful sets and
his splendid lighting design put every detail of the production in
relief. The ballet enjoyed several revivals over the following years,
before passing into oblivion, like many of my works. Most ballets
in the classical repertory had been passed on from one dancer to
the next. Only the invention of the videotape would finally make
it possible to record at least the steps of some of the dances that
could at best be reconstructed by a member of the company who
had danced in the piece. With luck, that person has been present
during its original choreographic process, as the choreographer's
instructions as to how the steps are to be executed are missing from
the dance being recorded. I personally believe that for a dance to
convey its original impact it needs the eyes and vocabulary of its
creator. The only other reliable way of reconstructing a dance is
one of the two established systems of dance notation, which the
company was never able to afford.

Prior to our move to the EJ Thomas Performing Arts Hall, John
and Barbara Schubert, two Clevelanders and supporters of all the
arts, discovered our work and would eventually become friends for
life. They were the first to commission a new work from me. The
ballet, *Badinage*, although only fifteen minutes long, contained some
new and technical challenges for its six dancers and remained in
the repertory for a number of seasons. Barbara had been the Junior
Committee chairperson of the Key Concerts for young people, ages
five through nine, of the Cleveland Orchestra. Determined to bring
the ballet and the orchestra together, she invited Mathias Bamert,
associate conductor of the Cleveland Orchestra, and myself to her
home. At that meeting, it became obvious that we had a strong
artistic connection, and I agreed to perform in the concert. Mathias

Bamert introduced me to an unusual composition by Sigfried Ochs. The composer had used the melody of an old German folk song and had arranged its theme in the styles of Mozart, Schubert, Wagner, and others, to hilarious effect. Unfortunately, there was not enough time for me to create a whole ballet to the music, and ultimately I used only three of the variations, which the company danced prior to my ballet *One Ring Circus,* to a score by Dmitry Kabalevsky, and a dance to the minuet from George Frederic Handel's *Water Music,* which were part of our existing repertory. In addition to having succeeded in creating a successful collaboration between Mathias Bamert and myself, Barbara had secured a grant from the Martha Holden Jennings Foundation to have the concert taped. At a later date, the program was aired on public TV stations around the country.

CHAPTER 21
Intermission

At the beginning of May 1976, I had to miss the opening performance of my ballet *Concerto Grosso*, to the music of the same title by Ernest Bloch. This has remained the only time I ever missed the opening performance of a ballet during my leadership of the company. Tom had brought me an audiotape he had made during the performance, so I would be able to judge its success by the audience's reaction. While listening to the tape, I was being prepared for surgery at the Cleveland Clinic. The following morning, I was to receive a double coronary bypass. Although I had met the surgeon and told him that my appearances as a dancer had long ago ended, he assured me that no scar would ever be detected from below the footlights after the healing process was completed. The surgeon's name was Paul Taylor, which had me thinking that if his work were as good as that of my friend the choreographer, I would surely wake up to start life all over again.

The very successful surgery was followed by several agonizing days and nights in a cold darkish dungeon. I woke with something that looked like the hose of a vacuum cleaner protruding from my mouth. A nurse was in charge of revolving a rotation device, sticking out from the hose, that when activated would produce violent coughs and pain. She was a very small woman wearing shoes with the highest heels, and the click-clack of her mincing steps had a very negative effect on my pained body and strained nerves. After several days, and when I was finally relieved of the hose, I talked to her about the effect the sound of her heels on the stone floor had had on me, and perhaps on others, too. She promised to dampen the sound in the future by having her heels covered with rubber pads.

After the removal of the hose from my lungs, it became necessary to employ the coughing technique we had learned as a group two days before surgery. This time, some hard punches on the back would produce the painful coughing spells all patients fear when being approached by those well-meaning but stern individuals in charge of such procedures. Finally, after I was rolled back into my room, things began to improve. The fact that I could feel and hear my own heartbeat made up for all the discomfort and pain associated with a bypass procedure at that time.

The end of the company's season had coincided with my surgery. Now dancers went on a lay-off period before returning for rehearsals four or five weeks later to prepare for our performances in the parks. The 1976 Summer Festival was followed by our first appearance in New York City at the Delacort Theater in Central Park with my ballet *Summer Night*, to the second movement of Chopin's Piano Concerto No. 2.

The ballet's success opened the doors for a week's engagement at the Jacob's Pillow Dance Festival in Lee, Massachusetts, in 1977. Under Norman Walker's directorship of the festival, Ohio Ballet would eventually perform several more seasons at the Pillow, which brought the company to the attention of the *New York Times*, the *Boston Globe*, and the *Village Voice*, among others.

At some time in 1977, it had become clear to me that the school I had founded with Kate Firestone in 1967 was suffering a major setback. My time had been consumed more and more with the growing needs of the company, which still consisted mostly of dancers I had trained personally. By now too much of the teaching had been entrusted to people who were unable to produce dancers good enough for the company. To solve the problem, Tom had arranged for a visit with Martha Hill, who was the head of the Dance Division of the Juilliard School in New York City. Ms. Hill had introduced herself to us when the company had performed in Jacob's Pillow. Together we probed into the possibility of bringing first one, and later maybe two ballet teachers from her school to Akron on a revolving basis. Our plans included classes to be held daily from late afternoons until evenings, instead of the still prevailing weekend classes only. We agreed in principle that Ms. Hill would investigate the possibilities while we, back in Akron, would prepare for the event of such a wonderful solution: professional teachers producing dancers for our and other companies under the aegis of the already existing university program.

After our return from New York, we discussed the plan with our general manager in the presence of Gena Carroll, who inquired at a certain point in the conversation about the position she was to attain by such a change. Tom answered for me, when he stated that nothing would change the role of the directorship for the school. Our general manager had composed a letter that would eventually reach the parents of students enrolled at the time. It stated in so many words that, in order to reorganize the school I had founded, classes would have to be suspended for a certain amount of time for students to be reauditioned at a yet unspecified time. The letter was sent immediately to the head of the Theater Arts Department of the university with the intention of bringing into discussion the possibility of expansion for such a venture at a mutually agreed time. In a letter addressed to me the following day, I was informed, by Dr. James F. Dunlap, Dean of the School of Fine and Applied Arts, that my actions had been out of order and that Mrs. Carroll had been assigned the directorship of the Dance Institute.

The mission of the school had always been to train young, gifted students for a career in dance, to be channeled upon graduation from high school into the university program. From here, the best students would eventually graduate to become members of the company, or audition for other companies. What I tried to do, however, was to find a loophole in the system that would enable me to accept only those students who had gone through previous ballet training and whose physical appearance would at least be a contributing factor for a career in classical ballet dancing. In short, it would be a professional school in an academic setting. That dream did not materialize, because the loophole I had spent much time trying to discover did not exist in the system and was looked upon as discriminatory for a number of overweight university students. I nonetheless dedicated all my efforts to the growth of Ohio Ballet as one of the best companies in the country with a style and personality of its own.

The Dance Department of the university had grown to a sizable number by now, with its faculty displaying a pronounced dislike of Ohio Ballet's presence in the same building. On several occasions, our general managers entertained the idea of searching for a building of our own. Some of our offices would be taken over by faculty members, including my own, which would leave me with no other place to be than in the studio at our assigned hours. Students of the Dance Department were always invited to watch the daily activities of our professional company and to attend classes. It turned out, and it was reported to me, that fraternization of that sort had been discouraged. I never really understood the reasons for those rejections and thought that perhaps our different goals or scheduling were to blame.

CHAPTER 22

Ohio Ballet's Breakthrough

During an extensive tour in 1979, which brought the company to Brooklyn College, Anna Kisselgoff in the *New York Times* declared Ohio Ballet to be "the best news in dance this season." Armed with such praise, we continued our sold-out tour through many cities in upstate New York and finally California, before returning east to the Jacob's Pillow Dance Festival.

That particular week at the Pillow seemed like a vacation to us after the many weeks of mostly one-night stands. The place was special. Everyone involved with the Pillow was committed to offer its patrons the best in dance that could be accommodated on its small stage in the Ted Shawn Theater. After performances, the owners of a late-night tavern would invariably go out of their way to prepare a meal from scratch, before we would retire very late at night to our motel-like compound.

When we returned to Akron, I received a phone call from Gian Carlo Menotti, the composer and founder of the world-renowned Festival of Two Worlds in Spoleto, Italy. Menotti asked for our participation at the Festival in 1980, which left me speechless but elated. I consulted with him about the programming for the visit, as our repertory contained a number of ballets by universally known choreographers, whose work I was eager to show on that occasion.

It turned out that Anna Kisselgoff's review in the *New York Times* had determined Menotti's decision that only my works comprise the two programs to be shown during our weeklong engagement. I ultimately chose two programs that would confirm Ohio Ballet's reputation as a chamber ballet company and present myself as essentially a romantic and a craftsman, at home in the classical idiom with a preferred tendency to the weight associated with modern dance.

During our week at the Festival of Two Worlds, the company danced to full houses and appreciative applause. We received a wonderful review in Rome's *Il Messagero*, but also a number of condescending comments from others. The smallness of the company took some of them by surprise, having expected a company the size of the state of Ohio. The festival's publicity department could have been at fault, but I suspect that its policy encourages surprising its audiences with the unexpected.

Stephen Ayers, for many years the general manager of the Children's Theater of Minneapolis, Minnesota, had joined Ohio Ballet that same year. Stephen's present to his newly wedded wife, Gail, was a trip to Italy, while he was functioning as our general manager. After the company returned to America, Stephen and Gail proceeded to spend the rest of their honeymoon in Venice and other places. The couple became close friends to Tom and me, and as such we were entrusted to be godfathers to their firstborn, Kelsey Anouk.

My oldest sister Änne with her two daughters Ursula and Gerda, plus their close friend Max, drove the distance from Munich to Spoleto for a visit with me and a chance to see what it was that had brought me and my company to Italy. Änne, who had moved from Oberhausen to München (Munich), had never in her life seen a dance performance and found the whole thing interesting because it made her speculate as to what part of the whole had been my responsibility.

For many years the company's touring schedule increased steadily. We criss-crossed the country from the north to the south and from the east to the west coasts, including Alaska and Hawaii. In 1986, the company embarked on a major tour of South America that included Argentina, Uruguay, Ecuador, Costa Rica, Panama, and Mexico. Our participation at the festival of Guanajuato, Mexico, proved to be an especially rewarding experience because of its week-long duration. With Tom's artistry and commitment on my side, we never, even under the most adverse circumstances, stopped working to improve on a performance. That held true wherever we happened to perform. Master classes in ballet and lighting were given during those tours, and we thrived on their demands. There were low points also, but mostly because of uncooperative sponsors or failing crews in some smaller cities in the Unites States, where ballet was not very high on the list of things to expend much effort on. Only Tom was able to convert a gymnasium into a temporary theater, which invariably elicited kudos from the sponsors. My major work on those tours consisted of teaching and guiding dancers through rehearsals and making them feel as comfortable and important as possible. During interviews, I always referred to them as professional men and woman who had chosen dance as a calling. Being perhaps the least profitable of the performing arts, dance, especially of the classical variety, requires an individual's absolute absorption of an unnatural set of rules necessary to qualify as a performer. Comments of that nature in most cases proved revelatory to the people assigned by their respective newspapers to write something in advance of a performance and would at times lead to articles that communicated valuable information to audiences about the lesser-known realities of our profession.

On the home front, at least among a few members of our board, there would occasionally be a voice that clamored for some fare that would be accessible to a larger audience. Of course, it was always wrongly presumed that if you filled the house, there would be no need to raise money for the operation of the company. In other words, something similar to the *Nutcracker*, if not the real thing, would solve all fundraising problems. However faint, Tom and I never capitulated to those suggestions, knowing that compared with the rest of our personal vision for the company, a production of such magnitude, with only sixteen dancers and three apprentices, would instantly mark as provincial what we had built so carefully. I have to mention here that Ohio Ballet was not a union company, and many of its board members grew visibly confused when confronted with the fact that being a professional dancer was a full-time job, although they had been told so repeatedly. Some trustees would even ask the dancers what they were doing for a living. It was always clear to us that a city the size of Akron would be able to sustain a small-scale company like ours, on par in terms of vision and overall artistry with the best in the country. We also always made it clear that if the board of trustees disapproved of our work, we would pick up our tent and leave for good. What kept us working in Akron was the joy we experienced when friends understood and approved of our work, and when other friends in New York, who had predicted disaster, realized that we were leading an important ballet company in Akron, Ohio.

New dancers would appear on our tours to audition or make the trip to Akron by car, train, or plane, from all corners of the country. It usually would take a whole season for a new member to feel comfortable with our working habits and be able to integrate into our approach to classical dancing. During the classes I taught, I would always comment on and demonstrate elements pertaining to different dance techniques, which I always used when making dances. In other classes, I would emphasize the strict and correct articulation of the academic vocabulary, especially the use of the feet. In addition to a strong technical base during auditions, I was always on the lookout for the dancer with a flair for movement that would reveal his or her distinct personality. A love of speed and understanding of how to make the music dance were also major influences on my decisions when hiring a dancer.

New members underwent their first test during our outdoor Summer Festival, which would serve to introduce them to our audiences in the parks. The company had always worked as a close-knit unit, instinctively making anyone who resisted integration into our ways leave the company voluntarily. Rare are the instances when I have personally been forced to terminate a dancer's contract. In most cases, it has been the dancer who, after having signed a contract, broke that contract during lay-off periods for better-paying jobs with other companies. It was never easy to recruit dancers for the company in Akron. Our salary levels were rarely on a level with other companies of our size and reputation, and many excellent dancers simply refused to move to the company's home base. Nonetheless, in many happy instances we have attracted gifted artists because of our hard-earned reputation and because of our many appearances in the vicinity of New York and finally at the Joyce Theater.

Being selected to participate in the Brooklyn Academy of Music's American Ballet Festival in 1981 gave the company an additional boost. We actually began to gain respect at home. Not that it made the public in Akron flock to the theater to see us, but we began to perceive a sense of respect for our accomplishments from the board of trustees and the university, whose association as the company's place of residence would attract students to its dance program.

The beginning of the eighties saw the city of Cleveland's process of revitalizing its downtown theater district. The previously rundown Ohio Theater proved to be the ideal size for our small company. For a long time, our friend Barbara Schubert had worked behind the scenes to make the company available to Cleveland audiences. In conjunction with our then general manager Stephen Ayers, and not without resistance from some members on our board, Barbara finally negotiated our first subscription series in 1982 at the newly restored Ohio Theater. The series continued with identical performances at EJ Thomas Performing Arts Hall and Ohio Theater on alternating weekends.

CHAPTER 23

A Change of Address

After several changes of residence in and around Akron, Tom and I purchased a small, charming house on one and a half acres of land with a man-made pond, about a half hour drive from the company's studio. Surrounded by mostly small family farms, we cultivated a garden that produced our own organically raised vegetables. Growing produce on our farm in New Jersey, as we had previously done, had by now become impossible because of the company's expanded Summer Festivals.

As a form of relaxation, amateur cooking had always been our favorite occupation, not just for friends, but also for our personal pleasure. On many occasions, we cooked for the benefit of a special group of Ohio Ballet supporters. For several years, the number of guests would reach into the eighties and always included company members, staff, and our crew. A tent would be erected in the event of rain; otherwise, the guests would feast while seated at rented tables covered with colorful tablecloths. An open bar in our garage supplied liquor, wine, and many kinds of soft beverages. In my memory, the event was never spoiled by rain; I only recall those days as perfectly sunny.

In 1975, Father had passed away after a very short illness. And now Mother, nine years later at the age of ninety-one, died in her sleep. I had visited her shortly before, and many years would pass before I would make it a point to visit both sisters every two or three years. Those visits would never exceed the span of one week, which included the time traveled from the United States to Germany and back home, and a day's trip from Oberhausen to Holzkirchen in the south, where my older sister lived. For as long as I can remember, my sisters had harbored a profound dislike of each other, and neither of them ever made an attempt at reconciliation. On my visits, mentioning one to the other would invariably lead to an unpleasant remark. Neither child of my older sister Änne ever mentioned another member of the family in unpleasant terms, while Else's daughter never had anything positive to report in answer to her mother's always negative remarks about her sister. My efforts at trying to make peace among them when I had visited in the early 1960s failed after I had left. In the end, I used to combine those visits with pleasure trips to Berlin, Venice, or Paris, to counteract the obligatory part of the journey. In 2000, my older sister Änne, for several years a victim of Alzheimer's, died in her sleep at the age of eighty-seven.

CHAPTER 24
Ohio Ballet's Golden Years

During the 1970s and 1980s, America experienced an unprecedented surge of interest in dance. Expanded tour schedules, made possible through the support of the National Endowment for the Arts, made dance performances on college campuses a major weekly event. Many colleges hosted no less than two dance events during a one-week period. Always well attended by a paying public and free to students, those performances seemed to be an ideal way to create an audience for the future. Dance performances actually attracted record numbers of patrons who had become curious about dance through the emergence of its superstars who had defected from the Soviet Union. At the same time, modern dance, which for such a long time had been an orphan in a world of ballet, began to push its collective weight into the American consciousness. In short, dance had become a major contributor to the entertainment industry and still maintains that status in some of America's biggest cities. Unfortunately for the companies that had established themselves over the years in smaller communities, and whose lifeblood depended upon touring to keep dancers dancing and paid for several more weeks during the seasonal contract, the news in the early nineties about the National Endowment for the Arts budget cuts practically severed any possibility for future touring. Already in

1988, the *Plain Dealer* in Cleveland had run a five-day series entitled "The Dark Side of Dance," which proved to have an adverse effect on Ohio Ballet. The series was directed at the leadership of the Cleveland and Ohio Ballets. The articles served no purpose except to scare people into believing their young children were being abused during their dance lessons and that all professional dancers were somehow emotionally scarred. At the time, it caused some otherwise dependable supporters to reduce or eliminate their funding. However, in time audiences came to understand that the making of professional dancers required the adherence to a series of highly specialized routines. After all, a ballet dancer has to work his or her body daily against nature to achieve the final results of the chosen art form.

Presenters who had received a major part of their expenses from the National Endowment for the Arts to bring dance or other performing arts attractions to their communities now found themselves having to make the choice between presentation of small-scale, much less expensive attractions, or ballet companies. Small dance companies like ours had sprung up all over the country, and competition for touring dates eventually became fierce. Lowering fees and cutting corners everywhere had become the norm, but ultimately nothing could renew the boom we had experienced before. A number of companies ventured into the presentation of large-scale story ballets, aimed at an audience that had come to prefer the spectacles of visiting Broadway shows. At the same time, a new breed of manager, in most cases forced by a board of trustees that was no longer attuned to the artistic director's vision, would try to reduce the role of artistic director to that of a ballet master. The artistic director's role in any performing arts organization has always included the shaping of that organization's artistic identity. Ohio Ballet, which we had nurtured to national prominence over many years, although highly respected by its presenters, became less affordable because repertory programs had lost their audience appeal. During the eighties and nineties, the company had matured. Paul Taylor's *Aureole* and *Three Epitaphs* had entered the repertory in the mid-seventies, to be joined by his *Big Bertha* in 1988. Other acquisitions during this period were *Concerto Barocco* and *Allegro Brilliante* by George Balanchine, together with Merce Cunningham's *Signals*, Pilobolus's *Untitled*, and Antony Tudor's *Dark Elegies*, to be followed by his *Judgment of Paris* in 1998. Kurt Jooss's *The Big City* had its Ohio Ballet premiere in 1994. Laura Dean, with whom the company had established a very special creative relationship, choreographed four distinguished dances that would for a long time remain high points in the company's repertory. Robert Joffrey's *Pas des Déesses*, Gerald Arpino's *Reflections*, *Photo Call* by Kathryn Posin, and, ultimately, Ruthanna Boris's *Cakewalk* had remained staples during the seventies, with *Cakewalk* receiving many revivals beyond that time. *Feral* by Molissa Fenley, *Code of Silence* and *In a Word* by Lynne Taylor-Corbett, *Another Way* by Charles Moulton and, finally, Donald Byrd's *Ellington Fantasia* complete the list of works by guest choreographers I acquired before my retirement from Ohio Ballet in 1999.

George Balanchine's *Concerto Barocco* had its premiere by Ohio Ballet in Boca Raton, Florida, during an intensive tour across that state in 1980. Balanchine's masterpiece graced our repertory for many years until, for reasons unknown to me, the right to continue to perform the work was denied by the person to whom Balanchine had willed the ballet after his death. The loss of *Concerto Barocco* as a measure of excellence for the company as a classically trained ensemble was a blow for me personally. After all, the ballet had been instrumental in affirming my faith in the art of classical choreography for our time when I had seen it performed by the New York City Ballet in Berlin in 1951.

Many of the dances I selected for inclusion in Ohio Ballet's repertory presented a challenge to our audiences at home. Cunningham's *Signals*, Taylor's *Big Bertha*, and even Tudor's *Dark Elegies* proved to be difficult for many of our patrons to classify as ballets. Fortunately, the press, in both Akron and Cleveland, always applauded the inclusion of works that would spark animated conversation and controversy. Although Paul Taylor's *Three Epitaphs* had three thousand children, bussed to the theater, in stitches and screaming with laughter, its subscription audience the following night received the dance with stupor and a sense of hostility.

During my thirty-one year leadership of Ohio Ballet, until Tom Skelton's untimely death in 1994 I was fortunate to enjoy his total support as cofounder, associate director, and eminent master lighting designer. Tom provided me with the space, the peace of mind, and the floor on which I could create over sixty works for the company. We built a perfectly harmonious and truly collaborative environment that always served as the base for Ohio Ballet's successes. For many years, Tom's work for the company did not include any financial compensation. His travels around the country for other companies always included air travel with stopovers in Akron or Cleveland, which saved the company the expense of having to pay for his trips. In later years, he received a small stipend for his work.

Support for our artistic vision was slow to appear, but thanks to financial help from friends like the late Ellen Herberich during our infant years and later John and Barbara Schubert and the Ohio Arts Council, we survived. Crucial support was also forthcoming through the University of Akron's generosity in providing the company with rehearsal and office space, and the National Endowment for the Arts' approval and support, which eventually led to a $250,000 matching grant.

Ohio Ballet's residency arrangement was meant to encourage students of dance from the university dance program to have access and firsthand understanding of the daily routine of a professional ballet company. For a number of years, the reigning faculty discouraged such involvement and participation on the grounds that my teaching methods and use of classical vocabulary were destructive to the students' health and bodies. Only a very few students saw the light and eventually accepted my invitation to attend classes with the company, which would let them join Ohio Ballet later. Fortunately, that relationship would change with the arrival of a different leadership at the Dance Department, which coincided with the company's reputation on the national and international scene.

CHAPTER 25

On Food and Travel

In 1989, Tom and I took our first vacation away from our yearly destination, the farm. We chose Italy. Since we were both enthusiastic pasta eaters, Italy seemed to be the logical destination. After having spent a week in Spoleto during Ohio Ballet's engagement there, and having tasted some delicious Italian food and wine, we prepared for a return visit. During the first three days, we ate ourselves through some of Venice's best culinary establishments. Having read about them in the many issues of food magazines strewn around the living room at the farm, we had made reservations at all of them before embarking on our two-week trip. To consume yet another meal, we dutifully walked over bridges, through a number of churches, the Guggenheim museum, the Doge's palace, and the Piazza San Marco, to end the day at Harry's Bar for drinks, before contentedly sitting down for another five-course dinner, wine, and the final prospect of a good night's sleep. Traveling by car from Venice, we drove through many beautiful little villages and towns, stopping for lunch in Vicenza and dinner in Verona, from where we left the following morning after breakfast for lunch in Mantova and our best and most sumptuous dinner in Modena at the restaurant Fini. Tom, through all of this, never gained an ounce. We proceeded to Ravenna for lunch and to Florence for dinner. In fact, we enjoyed several delicious lunches and dinners in Florence, the city we savored fully.

On arrival at our hotel there, Tom, being unable to shed his habit as a stage manager taking care of his crew, filled the bathtub with hot water into which he deposited all of our worn socks, underwear, and shirts, plus his favorite detergent, which he always carried with him. Because of his many travels around the country and overseas, his suitcase always contained a very generous supply of matches in addition to clothing, his beloved Picayune cigarettes, little pouches of sugar which he would invariably pocket from any restaurant table, and the occasional hotel towel. During his constant need for coffee at rehearsals, he never once found himself in need of sugar, and he would offer to share with anyone whenever the occasion arose.

Eventually, I left the hotel room, knowing that Tom would be washing our clothes for some time. We had agreed to meet an hour later on the steps of a nearby church from where we would speed by taxi to the restaurant that held our reservations. After dinner, when we returned to our hotel room, I found every available chair, table, and door decorated with dripping socks, underwear, and shirts.

We had to leave Florence after just a few days but not before we promised to return. The city and its treasures deserved a longer stay than we had scheduled on our present trip; contemplation of its many splendid artworks would have to take second place to our advanced restaurant bookings.

In Siena, we spent several hours tasting and buying wine at a local *enoteca*. The bottles of delicious dessert wines, intended for New Jersey, were gradually uncorked while we made our way through Perugia, Assisi, and finally Spoleto, before continuing our last stretch into Rome. We both had fallen in love with Italy, so sunny and unabashedly romantic, as opposed to the rest of Europe's austere beauty. The Sistine Chapel and the *Pietà* by Michelangelo were to us the undisputed high points in Rome. However, the vendors selling religious trinkets and postcards inside St. Peter's did nothing to reconfirm my faith in the church.

In 1992, during our second visit to Italy, I became aware of a major change in Tom's health. His heavy smoking had for a long time drawn comments from close associates in his field, in addition to his mother and myself. His desire to cut back, perhaps as a consequence of my insistence, had only resulted in his use of a filter when smoking his favorite brand of cigarettes. By now, the frequent coughing spells, after which he would in all innocence light yet another cigarette, caused me to suggest that he give hypnosis a try. In my own experience, after my double bypass operation in 1976, I had attributed the ability to stop smoking to the fact that my memory of having been a smoker had vanished completely, a theory which, although unconfirmed, I attributed to hypnosis. What else could have eliminated the desire to smoke again, and, more to the point, the memory of having ever enjoyed the act of inhaling the smoke from a cigarette? I will never know the truth, but could the idea of having experienced hypnosis during surgery be so farfetched? My consumption of cigarettes had amounted to three packs daily, and my many attempts to put an end to it had always been dismal failures. Those same failures haunted Tom, but my suggestion about hypnosis fell on sterile soil, to be followed by the lighting of another cigarette and the promise of a cutback. During this last visit to Italy, Tom's coughing spells worsened. He returned to New York to continue work on the designs for his current engagement. Arriving home from Paris a week later, I found Tom in his usual routine in front of his computer. After completion of another Ohio Ballet season, we returned to the farm to spend Christmas and New Year's Eve with friends and neighbors.

CHAPTER 26

1994

During our 1993 fall season at the Ohio Theater in Cleveland, Tom agreed to consult a doctor about his often excessive cough. Diagnosed as having bronchitis, he would swallow spoonfuls of anticough medicine prescribed for him. After the holidays, at the beginning of 1994, it seemed as if his condition had turned into a permanent fixture, and we decided that further tests were in order. In February of that year, Tom traveled to San Francisco to design the lighting for a new ballet by Helgi Tomasson, the artistic director of the San Francisco Ballet. He had not been feeling well and had asked my advice about cancelling his commitment. Knowing Tom, I reminded him that he would never forgive himself if he cancelled. I knew that this was the answer he needed and wanted to hear. He left with a slight fever and called me late that night to tell me that he was very tired, ready to fall asleep. He subsequently left San Francisco after the dress rehearsal to take the red-eye back to Ohio. After several more days, it became obvious that his condition was not improving. His persistent, slightly elevated fever worried us. The next day's visit to the clinic revealed nothing new, but he was urged to report back if his temperature did not subside within a few more days and after a more aggressive treatment with antibiotics.

At the same time, I had detected a persistent nagging and numb discomfort in the right side of my lower back, reminiscent of the feeling I had had when another kidney stone was discovered and removed, at the beginning of 1979. During Tom's next visit to the clinic, I called on the doctor who was familiar with my history there, which resulted in a few tests that revealed an elevated PSA level. A subsequent biopsy of my prostate gland turned out positive, and the decision was made for radiation treatment. Fortunately, the tumor had been discovered in its earliest stage. The five weekly visits to the Akron City Hospital, just a few blocks from our ballet studios, where our mutual radiation therapy would eventually take place, were made without anybody's knowledge about my personal condition. My concern centered exclusively on Tom's illness. He finally had been diagnosed with lung cancer and with only a four-to six-month life expectancy. This news, given to us suddenly during a visit with an oncologist, propelled me into a kind of stupor, resulting in a minor car accident that I caused when we left the hospital. I still believe that Tom hadn't grasped the seriousness of it all when his initial reaction was to inquire of the doctor how many times during any given day he had to deliver such bad news. The doctor, taken by surprise by Tom's inquiry, finally admitted that telling patients the truth was part of his daily work.

During the following two months, I sensed that Tom was in denial at times. He seemed determined to gain weight by eating copious breakfasts, lunches, and dinners. Throughout Tom's illness, my time was spent caring for him and preparing for the inevitable. My major concern centered on the intention that no physical pain would mar a peaceful passing. The diagnosis had also revealed that the disease had spread to the bones. The work on his computer, mostly instructions about Ohio Ballet's light plots, had become more and more difficult because of the pain in his right arm. Surgical removal of the cancer from his arm made it possible to continue his function on the computer. Some of his instructions were made in the car, in a parking lot across from the studio, to the company's technical director, while I would spend time looking in on Anna Markard's staging of Kurt Jooss's *Big City*. Throughout our ordeal, Anna, Jooss's daughter, was always understanding about my many absences from rehearsals and handled the situation with perfect professionalism. Finally, Tom's presence at the lighting and dress rehearsal, together with Herman Markard, Anna's husband and designer for the lighting and costumes of Jooss's ballet, would be his last in the Ohio Theater with the company he had cofounded twenty-six years earlier.

In spite of continued radiation therapy, designed only to slow the disease, which by now had metastasized to his brain, Tom's condition worsened at an alarming rate. His confinement to a wheelchair made it still possible for him to be moved from my bedroom, where a hospital bed had been installed, through part of the house and to a screened-in porch, where he liked to linger most of the day. Julie Duro, who later became the company's lighting designer until my retirement, provided Tom with the help he needed to organize his professional work, especially the lighting he had created for Ohio Ballet. Three days before his death on August 9, 1994, our friends John and Barbara Schubert managed to drive Tom to Firestone Park, where Ohio Ballet was in performance at its yearly outdoor Summer Festival. The car, situated in such a way that Tom could witness the performance of Paul Taylor's *Aureole*, served as a place where he took leave of close friends. Kelsey Smogard-Ayers, our godchild, who was celebrating her eleventh birthday, had traveled with her parents, Stephen and Gail, from Minneapolis to spend a few precious hours with us. Several weeks earlier, with Tom still in control of performances in a different park, Laura Dean and Ellen Kogan had come from New York to bid farewell as soon as word had reached them, and so had Jennifer Tipton and Tom's agent, Micky Rolfe. Louise Guthman, another longtime friend and Ohio Ballet supporter, had come from Columbus.

By now, Tom had been on oxygen for several days, but that morning of August 9, he begged me to increase the pressure, which I did with the cooperation of the head nurse from the palliative care unit who had become a constant presence.

For the last month, I had been able to move Tom into the shower where his weakened state had made it impossible for him to stand and wash himself. During his last days, although he insisted on being wheeled to the nearby toilet facility every morning, he finally consented that I wash him while he lay in bed. On this, his last day, he fell asleep shortly afterward but still managed to mention that he had to do much work later. I stayed at his bedside for several hours, holding his hand, until I felt that he had ceased to respond to my touch. I immediately reported to the head nurse, who urged me to stay and talk to him. With every word I spoke, his breathing became more agitated. Tom died at four o'clock in the afternoon. At the moment of his death, I witnessed the transformation of this once so vibrant and creative man into a shell. Only then did I realize that Tom had gone, the person with whom I had shared thirty years of unconditional love, respect, and complete trust. My grief has never lessened, but I have been able to convert that grief into the positive asset that is life itself.

CHAPTER 27
Exit

The fall of 1994 marked the preparation of Ohio Ballet's season
at the Joyce Theater in New York City the following February 1995.

Everything had fallen into the usual rhythm of classes, rehearsals, and performances, and the season at home and in New York
proved successful and invigorating for the company. However,
touring had become practically nonexistent by now, and contracts,
which had at one time extended to forty-two weeks, would subsequently be shortened to thirty-eight, thirty-six, and ultimately
thirty-two weeks. The demand for one-act ballets had lessened, and
would in time further diminish, while full-evening works were in
demand everywhere. Although I was fully aware of the situation, my
interest in dance had never expanded into the sphere of mere popular entertainment. The works now offered to me by other choreographers, who specialized in those spectacles, would have destroyed
the uniqueness of the company Tom and I had built according to
our vision. For some time, it had become clear to me that this vision
was to be less and less shared by the leadership of the company's
board of trustees. The company's profile would eventually deteri-
orate if I were to follow the wishes and ultimate demands of the
board's leadership. Although the company's early efforts to dance
at the Joyce Theater and on its extensive tours had the support of

the board, our appearance in New York in February 1998 under my direction, our most successful yet, marked the first time that no member of the board of directors was present at the performances. No congratulatory note or telegram and virtually no response to very positive reviews made dancers and staff wonder about the state of affairs in Akron. The lack of encouragement and total failure to comprehend Ohio Ballet's mission statement by the leader of the board began to inform my decision to leave the company. Although I knew that a vision and its mission is not something boards of arts organizations specialize in, I finally, and after much deliberation, decided that my retirement would avoid controversy.

My retirement from the University of Akron and subsequently Ohio Ballet became effective on June 1, 1999, and with it an important chapter of my life had ended. I left a number of my ballets to long-time members of the company, and some of those works have found life with other companies. Do I miss what I left behind? Yes, I miss a number of gifted dancers and other individuals I worked with for thirty-one years. Did I make mistakes? Of course, I did. I had choreographed over sixty ballets for the company, and with some of them I didn't succeed. And, in spite of all the hardships associated with touring, especially the one-night stands and long bus rides, I miss those years. The dancers would usually sleep on those trips, play cards, knit, read, or, whenever the bus had a television hanging from the ceiling, watch their favorite movies. It was on one of those bus rides, somewhere in the Midwest, that I began writing the story you are reading right now. I also very much miss the criss-crossing of the country that has become my home. Those trips taught me much about Americans, the gentleness of the people and the love of their country. There is also nothing more satisfying for a director of any arts organization than having achieved a successful interaction between its artists and the person who is responsible for leading them. I also miss the many faithful people who comprised our audiences and, of course, the ones who worked in our offices. You are and always were my family. I miss your devotion to our common course, your so often all-night work during the 1980s, and I miss your interest and interaction with the company's artists. The strength of that bond has helped me overcome the occasional adversity that sometimes threatened the future of Ohio Ballet.

It is wintry and cold outside. Eight inches of snow have fallen overnight. The blinding white, marked by imprints from passing deer, rabbits, and other familiar furry critters, signals the beginning of a new slate of events. Christmas passed quietly, and it is just a few more days before the dawning of a new millennium. My life seems always to have been a series of shadows and light, to be interrupted by my arrival in the United States of America in 1964, which I consider the beginning of my "Light Years." This has become my home, where I have found friendship, family, and love, the missing link that had prevented my own father and mother from ever saying, "I love you, son," which robbed me of the opportunity to respond, "I love you, too."

Stockton, NJ
December 27, 1999

Choreography by Heinz Poll
for Ohio Ballet

1968
Micro Concerto (Albinoni)
Elegiac Song (Shostakovich)*
Rossiniana (Rossini)

1969
Compulsions (Rosenthal)
Nocturnes (Field)
Preface (Britten)

1970
Pantomime I & II (Saint-Saëns)
Spring Equinox '70 (Mozart, Freiberg, Duncan)
Royal Divertissement (Handel)

1971
One-Ring Circus (Kabalevsky)
. . . a time to dance (Jefferson Airplane)
The Witch (Shoenberg)

1972
Soirées Musicales (Britten)
Reminiscence (Lake)
Symphonic Dances (Rachmaninoff)

1973
Adagio For Two Dancers (Albinoni)*
Badinage (Vivaldi)
Saastras (McPhee)

1974
Summer Night (Chopin)*
Galante Taenze (Mozart)

1975
Schubert Waltzes (Schubert)*
Mysterious Mountain (Hovhaness)

1976
Concerto Grosso (Bloch)*
Twilight of Birches (Arensky)

1977
Scenes From Childhood (Schumann)*
On an Off Day (Vivaldi)

1978
Pavane (Fauré)*
Vienna Variations (Lanner, J. Strauss, Jr.)
Fantasy in F Minor (Schubert)*

1979
Primavera (Corelli)
Duet (J. S. Bach)*

1980
Ode (Brahms)
Dance Suite (Avison)
Images (Debussy)

1981
Lyric Divertissement (Schumann)
Wings and Aires (J. S. Bach)*

1982
Songs Without Words (Mendelssohn)*
Excursions (Pace)

1983
Fresco (Beethoven)
Tristeza (Barrios)
The Match Girl (Rydberg)

1984
Undercurrents (Chavez)
Called Back–Emily (Barber)
Light Breeze (Sanborn)*

1985
Cascade (J. S. Bach, Handel)*
Summoned Echoes (Scriabin)

1986
Horizons (Berkeley)
Concert Dances (J. S. Bach)

1987
Orfeo ed Eurydice (Glück)
Games (Mozart)

1988
Triptych (Mendelssohn)**
Faerie-Tale (Gounod)

1989
Essays (Sanborn)

1990
Planes/Configurations (Reich)*

1991
Brandenburg (J. S. Bach)

1992
Eight by Benny Goodman (arr. Goodman)*
Andante Nobilissima (van Wassenaer)

1993
Rococo Variations (Tchaikovsky)*

1994
In Full Swing (arr. Goodman)*

1996
Bolero (Ravel)*
Jungle Book [in collaboration with V. P. Shanta Dhananajayan]
    (Rao)
At Dusk (Schumann)

1997
Moonlight Serenade (arr. Miller)

1998
Elysian Fields (J. C. Bach)

*Heinz Poll gave the right to set these works for companies capable
of performing them to dancers who performed the pieces while they
were members of Ohio Ballet.

**The middle section of this ballet was given to a dancer, with the
right to set it for companies capable of performing it, using the title
Andante Sostenuto.

Index

Index

Brecht, Bertolt, 93
Brintz, Jutta, 91, 121, 132
British: diplomat, 101–2; embassy, 98;
  sector, 92, 97; soldiers, 60, 73, 74
Broadway, 127, 133, 149, 150, 151, 153,
  165; shows, 134, 184
Brooklyn Academy of Music's
  American Ballet Festival, 179
Bruhn, Eric, 127, 136
Buenos Aires, Argentina, 96, 114,
  117–19, 123, 128, 133
Bunster, Patricio, 104–5, 108–9, 134
Burbridge, Edward, 134, 148
Byrd, Donald, 185
Byrne, Anne, 143

Calaucan, 134
Capriccio Español, 87
Carmen, 80, 155
Carmina Burana, 111, 131, 134
Carnegie Hall, 136, 138–39
Carroll, Dr. Bill, 156, 167
Carroll, Gena, 156–57, 167, 173
Casino de Paris, 126
Cebron, Jean, 109
Celebrations, 140
Chamber Ballet, xiii, 158, 160, 162,
  165–67
Champion, Gower, 153
Chaplin, Geraldine, 124–25
Charrat, Janine, 127
Childs, Lucinda, viii
Chile, 95–97, 99–100, 104, 109, 113,
  122–23, 125, 129, 131; Chileans,
  104, 106, 135
Chilean National Ballet. See National
  Ballet of Chile
Chilean Embassy (Frankfort), 99; at
  Christmas, 7, 104, 119
Cinderella, 124
Cintolesi, Octavio, 105, 108
City Center Theater, 150
Cleveland Ballet, 184

Cleveland Orchestra, xiv, 169
Cocteau, Jean, 127
Code of Silence, 185
Concertino, 116
Concerto Barocco, 95, 164, 185
Concerto Grosso, 171
Coppelia, 111
Cranko, John, 88
Croqueuse de diamants, La, 125
Crumrine, Christine, 160
Cuevas, Marquis de, 115, 124, 129
Cullberg, Birgit, 116
Cunningham, Merce, viii, 185–86

Dakar, West Africa, 102, 119
Dark Elegies, viii, 185–86
Damase, Jean Michel, 125–26, 131
Dämon, Der, 88
Dance Library of Israel, 138
dance notation, 169
Dances at a Gathering, 151
Danilova, Alexandra, Madame, 136–37
Danton, Henry, 143, 145
Dean, Laura, viii, 185, 193
Deege, Gisela, 93–94
Delacort Theater, 158, 172
De Mille, Agnes, 151
Denmark, 33, 35–37
Design for Strings, 116, 129
Deutsches Schauspielhaus, 93
Deutsches Theater, 77, 88–89
Dido and Aeneas, 78–80
Dijk, Peter van, 94
Divertimento Real, 115
Don Quixote, 94
Don Juan, 104
Dooley, Dennis, xvii
Dornröschen, 94
Duncan, Isadora, 119
Dunlap, Dr. James F., 162, 173
Dunning, Jennifer, xvii
Duro, Julie, 193
Dusseldorf, Germany, 3, 119

Series on Ohio History and Culture

George W. Knepper, *Summit's Glory*

Leonard Sweet, *Strong in the Broken Places*

John H. White and Robert J. White Sr., *The Island Queen*

H. Roger Grant, *Ohio's Railway Age in Postcards*

Frances McGovern, *Written on the Hills: The Making of the Akron Landscape*

Keith McClellan, *The Sunday Game: At the Dawn of Professional Football*

Steve Love and David Giffels, *Wheels of Fortune: The Story of Rubber in Akron*

Alfred Winslow Jones and Daniel Nelson, *Life, Liberty, and Property:
A Story of Conflict and a Measurement of Conflicting Rights*

David Brendan Hopes, *A Childhood in the Milky Way: Becoming a Poet in Ohio*

John Keim, *Legends by the Lake: The Cleveland Browns at Municipal Stadium*

Richard B. Schwartz, *The Biggest City in America: A Fifties Boyhood in Ohio*

Thomas A. Rumer, *Unearthing the Land: The Story of Ohio's Scioto Marsh*

Steve Love, Ian Adams, and Barney Taxel, *Stan Hywet Hall & Gardens*

William F. Romain, *Mysteries of the Hopewell: Astronomers, Geometers, and
Magicians of the Eastern Woodlands*

Dale Topping, edited by Eric Brothers, *When Giants Roamed the Sky: Karl
Arnstein and the Rise of Airships from Zeppelin to Goodyear*

Millard F. Rogers Jr., *Rich in Good Works: Mary M. Emery of Cincinnati*

Frances McGovern, *Fun, Cheap, & Easy: My Life in Ohio Politics, 1949–1964*

Larry L. Nelson, editor, *A History of Jonathan Alder: His Captivity and Life
with the Indians*

Bruce M. Meyer, *The Once and Future Union: The Rise and Fall of the United
Rubber Workers, 1935–1995*

Steve Love and Ian Adams, *The Holden Arboretum*

Joyce Dyer, *Gum-Dipped: A Daughter Remembers Rubber Town*

Melanie Payne, *Champions, Cheaters, and Childhood Dreams: Memories of the Soap Box Derby*

John Flower, *Downstairs, Upstairs: The Changed Spirit and Face of College Life in America*

Wayne Embry and Mary Schmitt Boyer, *The Inside Game: Race, Power, and Politics in the NBA*

Robin Yocum, *Dead Before Deadline: . . . And Other Tales from the Police Beat*

A. Martin Byers, *The Ohio Hopewell Episode: Paradigm Lost and Paradigm Gained*

Edward C. Arn, edited by Jerome Mushkat, *Arn's War: Memoirs of a World War II Infantryman, 1940–1946*

Brian Bruce, *Thomas Boyd: Lost Author of the "Lost Generation"*

Kathleen Endres, *Akron's "Better Half": Women's Clubs and the Humanization of a City, 1825–1925*

Russ Musarra and Chuck Ayers, *Walks Around Akron: Rediscovering a City in Transition*

Heinz Poll, edited by Barbara Schubert, *A Time to Dance: The Life of Heinz Poll*